The Passion

Paul Thigpen

with a foreword by Holly McClure

Allegiance Press, Inc.

WASHINGTON, D.C.

Allegiance Press
10640 Main Street
Suite 204
Fairfax, VA 22030
www.allegiancepress.com

(703) 934-4411

Excerpts from the works of Maria de Agreda were freely translated, adapted, and abridged by Paul Thigpen from Maria de Jesús, *Mystica ciudad de Dios, milagro de su omnipotencia, y abysmo de la gracia* ... (Madrid: Imprenta de la Causa de la V. Madre, 1744).

Excerpts from Anne Catherine Emmerich were freely adapted and abridged by Paul Thigpen from the 20th edition of the English translation of the German original by Clemens Brentano, *The Dolorous Passion of Our Lord Jesus Christ According to the Meditations of Anne Catherine Emmerich* (New York: Benziger Brothers, 1904).

❦

"He who desires to go on advancing from virtue to virtue, from grace to grace, should meditate continually on the Passion of Jesus...There is no practice more profitable for the entire sanctification of the soul than the frequent meditation on the sufferings of Jesus Christ."

- St. Bonaventure

For Mel Gibson

His faith, fortitude, and vision inspire us all

CONTENTS

Contents

Foreword

꧁꧂

*H*ow do you capture in words a spiritual event that sets in motion a new track for your career—and winds up changing you to the core? That's the problem I faced as I sat down to write the introduction for this book, *The Passion*, an ink-and-paper companion to the epic film by Mel Gibson on the last twelve hours of Christ. Because, you see, the story of my involvement with the filming of Gibson's masterpiece began innocuously enough, like most seismic shifts in a person's spiritual journey.

For me, it all started with a grudging letter and a surprise phone call. The letter, prompted by the Holy Spirit, was an act of forgiveness to someone who had wounded me over a long period of time. Though I tried to argue with God about it, I ended up crafting those words of forgiveness and sending the letter off.

There, it's done, I thought as I put the unwanted task behind me. In doing so, I unwittingly opened a door in the spirit realm for God to bless me with a new task—one that would change my life and become my "Esther" moment. That afternoon I received a phone call from Mel Gibson's assistant, informing me that the famous actor and director would like to meet with me the following day to discuss his upcoming movie about Christ.

As a Christian movie critic, my work frequently takes me into film studios and onto movie sets, but I had never been prepared for the experience that awaited me in Italy, where Gibson filmed *The Passion of the Christ.* As I look back on the events that unfolded, I can't help but smile at the irony of God, who is in the business of changing people more than any other endeavor on earth. The lesson of forgiveness was to be the very theme of Gibson's movie that I was about to become a part of, for truly *The Passion* is about God's greatest gift of love and the greatest act of forgiveness the world has ever known.

The Passion is Mel Gibson's labor of love. A project that has taken him more than twelve years to write, produce, direct, and now distribute, the story focuses on the final hours of Jesus' earthly life, beginning with His betrayal, arrest, trial, and conviction and culminating with His graphic crucifixion and resurrection from the tomb. Jim Caviezel (*The Count of Monte Cristo*) plays Jesus, Romanian actress Maia Morgenstern portrays Jesus' mother Mary, and the beautiful Italian actress Monica Bellucci (*The Matrix: Reloaded*) plays Mary Magdalen.

Mel Gibson is actually a shy person who doesn't like to be interviewed by the press. A humble man, he is at the same time fully aware of the effect his star status has on most people and quick to down-play his "Hollywood royalty" image by making whomever he meets feel comfortable with his wonderful sense of humor.

Shortly after I visited his office and was invited to go on location with the cast and film crew, he gave me a copy of the script and told me he would call from Rome for my opinion of it. Two weeks later I received a trans-Atlantic call from Gibson, asking if there were any changes I would make to the script. One thing in particular troubled me, I told him: the issue of Mary Magdalen. Throughout the entire movie, Mary Magdalen is in every scene with Mary (the mother of Jesus) and clearly adores Jesus, to the point of wiping His blood with her hair. "But who is she, Mel?" I asked gently but boldly. "Is she His sister? His wife? A lover? You have to pretend no one knows the story of Jesus and why this woman would follow Him faithfully, risking life and death."

After a pause, he said matter-of-factly, "You're right, Holly. I've been working on this script for almost nine years, and no one has ever pointed that out to me. I need to show a flashback to connect her relationship to Him." I smiled and said, "It takes a woman's touch to see that she needs an introduction so people don't get the wrong idea about your film. You don't want people to assume the wrong thing about Mary. Maybe you could add a scene like the one where the people are going to stone a woman caught in adultery and—"

"Yes, and Jesus steps in and saves her!" Gibson blurted, his deep voice excited and brimming with a word picture of how he would film the sequence. "I'll show the guys dropping the stones one by one, and Mary looking up at Jesus!" It was a moment I'll never forget, and the scene is one of my favorites in the movie.

When I visited the set in December 2002, I was in awe as I drove through the historic sites of Rome, past the ancient ruins of the baths of Caracalla, past the infamous Christian Catacombs, and through the Italian countryside to the legendary Cinecitta studios. I was struck by the irony of Gibson creating a movie about the passion of Christ in the very city that was intrinsically linked with Christ's crucifixion over two thousand years ago. I literally pinched myself as a reminder that I was called here for a purpose, "for such a time as this."

As I passed through the gates of Cinecitta and

drove to the back lot, Mel Gibson's Jerusalem rose into view alongside the decaying sets of Martin Scorsese's *Gangs of New York*. Spanning two and a half acres, the breathtaking spectacle of biblical proportions consisted of giant columns, flights of stone steps, massive wooden temple doors, and Pilate's palace, where Jesus would be judged and beaten.

The first night I walked on the set (they were shooting night scenes) Gibson stood in the courtyard of his massive Jewish temple, bathed in golden lights with the evening stars overhead. He laughed with his crew while wearing a red clown nose and discussing directions in between scenes. Gibson enjoys using comic relief, such as wearing a clown nose, to make those he works with feel at ease and to keep the mood on the set relaxed and cheerful (especially when dealing with heavy scenes).

For a month I observed Mel Gibson direct, produce, and create his biblical masterpiece, pouring his heart, health, emotions, talent, and faith into every scene. I was not only impressed with the entire production and beauty of the film but was changed by my encounter with it. "I'm doing what I've always done," Gibson says of the movie. "I'm telling a story I think is important in the language I speak best: film. Most great stories are hero stories. People want to reach out and grab at something higher and vicariously live through heroism, and lift their spirit that way." And, he admits, there's no greater adventure story to tell than this one. "It's one of the biggest love stories to tell—God becoming man and sending His Son to love and forgive those who kill Him. That's about the greatest love one can have, to lay down one's life for someone."

Raised in the Catholic Church, Mel Gibson considers himself a traditionalist and a lover of the high Roman Mass. His rowdy days of early celebrity status and the lifestyle that went with it are long gone. His reputation these days is that of a brilliant actor/director whose devotion to his family and faith is shared only by his passion for making movies. In fact, he confided to me that he may not continue acting because he loves being "behind the camera" so much.

Although we live in a postmodern, post-Christian world, Gibson is still amazed that many people don't know the story of Jesus. "People kind of know generally what happened to Jesus, but they don't have an idea of what had to come together in order for His crucifixion to happen. Politics and religion were involved—Pilate's dilemma, Caiphas' jealousy, the fickleness of the people, and what went on between Jesus and His disciples. My story will demand a certain knowledge of the last few hours of Christ's life, but it's a different way of telling the story, and I think [the film] is more poignant for that reason."

Gibson co-wrote his script with screenwriter Ben Fitzgerald (*Wise Blood*), taking the plot directly from Scripture in the Gospels of Matthew, Mark, Luke, and John, or, as he likes to joke, "four obscure writers." He also researched an old book in his library, *The Dolorous Passion of Our Lord Jesus Christ*, written by nineteenth-century nun Anne Catherine Emmerich. "The book practically jumped off the shelf at me," Gibson says. "I bought this old library of books with some old tomes in there, and I reached up for a title and pulled it out, and the one next to it fell into my hands, so I started reading it."

But why would Mel Gibson want to make this movie in the first place? What was going on in his life to prompt him to write this kind of script? He tells it best in his own words: "When I was growing up, the whole story of the Passion was very sanitized and distant. It seemed to me very much like a fairy tale. Then from about the age of fifteen to age thirty-five, I kind of did my own thing. I still believed in God; I just didn't practice my faith or give it much consideration. I went through that period in life where you put a lot of other things first. So, coming back twenty years later and looking at Christ and what He went through, it seemed distant. I had to reconsider and say to myself, 'This wasn't a fairy tale; this actually happened. This was real.' And that started me thinking about what it must have been like, what Christ must have gone through. That's when the idea started to percolate inside my head. I began to see it realistically, re-creating it in my own mind so that it would make sense for me, so I could relate to it. And that's what I've tried to put on the screen."

Much controversy centers on the fact that Gibson chose to do his film in Aramaic, but for this down-to-earth director it's all about the demand for authenticity. The effect of hearing this ancient language spoken against the lifelike sets of "Jerusalem" is powerful, and I was caught up in the drama despite my ignorance of the language. As Jim Caviezel ("Jesus") spoke his lines I often closed my eyes and imagined Jesus standing in front of me. It was like being transported back in time. Gibson realizes that watching a film in another language may not appeal to everyone, and he takes it in stride. "Not everybody's going to like it, but that's okay," he says. "It's done with the right spirit, and that's what counts."

As the days turned into weeks, an interesting phenomenon took place on and off the set. People started reporting miraculous occurrences, things that couldn't be accounted for by anything other than the supernatural. "There is an interesting power in the script, so a lot of unusual things were happening, good things like people being healed of diseases, a couple of people who had their sight and hearing restored, another guy who was struck by lightning during the crucifixion scene and just got up and walked away," says Caviezel. He marvels at how the movie has touched most of the cast in some deep and personal way. "What seems to be happening because of this movie really gives you a lot of hope," he adds. "I mean, we're not kidding around about this—it's really happening."

To portray the most famous Man that ever lived requires an actor who is confident, controlled, and able to radiate a look of mercy, love, and forgiveness through his eyes. Gibson knew Jim Caviezel could do just that. "Jim has a quality about him—a divine light around him, an innocence," Gibson says. The six-foot-two actor is strikingly handsome with black hair, a radiant smile, and blue eyes that seem to penetrate your thoughts with just a glance. I pointed out to Caviezel that he and Christ share the same initials, JC. He smiled knowingly and replied, "Last year when Mel asked me to play the part I said to him, 'Do you realize I'm 33 years old, the same age Jesus was when He went through all of this?'"

Caviezel speaks softly but has strong convictions about life and playing what he considers the most important role of his lifetime. He took the role seriously—daily going to Mass, praying, and carrying several crucifixes and medallions in a pocket of his loincloth. He even got an audience with the pope. One of those rare actors who practice what they preach, he refuses to do sex scenes with his co-stars and will walk off the set if a director tries to break his contract and force him to do a nude scene. Although that doesn't make him a popular actor in Hollywood, he doesn't seem to mind. "I know I have that reputation, but I don't care," Caviezel says. "My career is not guided by those in Hollywood anyway. I honestly believe God gave me this career, and I feel He has blessed me and makes choices for me."

On an average shooting day, Caviezel went through an arduous makeup session that lasted from four to seven hours, transforming his clean-shaven face into a believable image of Jesus through the different stages of His arrest and crucifixion. Even Gibson was amazed one day when he saw Caviezel on camera. "He looks like the Shroud of Turin!" Gibson exclaimed. As for his performance, Caviezel believes it was truly inspired. "I'm interested in letting God work through me to play this role. I believe the Holy Spirit has been leading me in the right direction and [encouraged me] to get away from my own physical flesh and allow the character of Jesus to be played out the way God wants it— that's all I can do."

Most people cannot imagine what Jesus really went through in His last hours on earth, but Caviezel has a fair idea. "I was spit on, beaten, and I carried my cross for days over and over the same road," he says. "It was brutal. Mel likes to put violence in his movies, but the fact is they represent truth. All Mel cares about is making it look true to the text. No time has a film of our Lord ever been shown like this one. Believe me, when people get to the crucifixion scene, many won't be able to take it and will have to walk out. But I believe there will be many who will stay and be drawn to the truth."

The violence in *The Passion* is the topic that seems to draw the most media attention, but once again Gibson emphasizes that this is an event that actually happened. "I'm exploring it this way, I think, to show the extent of the sacrifice willingly taken by Jesus," Gibson says. "The price He paid is as much a part of what Jesus went through as the resurrection." The special-effects team of makeup artists and technicians were challenged to devise new ways of creating realistic crucifixion and flagellation scenes. They also devised a never-done-before technique of showing the nails being driven into Christ's hands, and, yes, it looks real. Although the scenes of Christ's torture are difficult to watch, as a Christian I clearly saw for the first time what Calvary really meant and what Jesus must have suffered. It strengthened my faith and made me grateful for the price He paid.

Though the movie focuses on the last twelve hours Christ spent on this earth, Gibson has added other scenes to familiarize audiences with Jesus' life and ministry. For instance, when Jesus is stumbling under the weight of the cross, Mary flashes back to when Jesus was a boy and fell down. Gibson also added bits and pieces of the Last Supper, Jesus washing the apostles' feet, and other scenes to make it all gel together.

"This is a very personal story for everyone," Gibson states. "Every nation and every creed has been influenced by Christ in some way or another, and everyone has differing opinions about who He is, what He is, and why, or whether they even believe Him or not. And that's the point of my film, really, to show all that turmoil around Him politically and with religious leaders and the people, all because He is who He is. This isn't a story about Jews vs. Christians. Jesus Himself was a Jew, His mother was a Jew, and so were His twelve apostles. It's true that, as the Bible says, 'He came unto his own and his own received him not,' I can't hide that."

In fact, Gibson points out that as a society, we all are culpable. "When you look at the reasons behind why Christ came—why He was crucified—He died for all mankind and He suffered for all mankind. So really anybody who sins has to look at their own culpability. We all pretty much know this isn't the usual theology of Hollywood."

Gibson claims he was "moved by the Holy Spirit" while directing *The Passion*, and he asserts that the film is ultimately about faith, hope, love and forgiveness. He also readily admits he's been changed by the experience. "Dwelling on this subject matter day in and day out and being involved in it all the time really begins to inhabit you—but I see that as a good thing," Gibson says. "You start to realize the value of life and keeping your temper in check, or the value of forgiveness even when people are doing things that wrong you. This is a story that has inspired art, culture, behavior, governments, kingdoms, countries—it has influenced the world in more ways than you can imagine. Believers and nonbelievers alike, we have all been affected by it. Jesus Christ is undoubtedly one of the most important historical figures of all time. Name one person who has had a greater impact on the course of history."

Long after moviegoers leave the theater, Gibson hopes the story of *The Passion* will captivate them as it did him. "My hope is that this movie will affect people on a very profound level and somehow change them. There's so much turmoil in the world today. When the world is tried in this way, people usually start going back to something higher to fill a void in their souls. I don't think there's a better message you could put out there than what's in this movie. Jesus suffered for all of us and He died for mankind. We could all use a little more love, faith, hope, and forgiveness, don't you think?"

I have watched *The Passion* several times now because I produced and directed a "making of" documentary about the movie and created several production pieces from the film for promotional purposes. When the movie ended I couldn't speak for several moments because I was so touched by the powerful images and incredible performances. Without question, it is one of the most visually moving experiences most people will ever see. And it is one of the most profound statements about God's love for all mankind, no matter who they are or where they've come from. No one can see this film and ever look at the sacrifice paid on the cross the same way again. And who could go through the motions on Easter morning, taking for granted what Christ suffered on that cross?

I predict *The Passion* is going to change millions of lives. Mel Gibson was correct when he said the Holy Spirit was the real director and he as a man was simply being obedient to God. When you see the movie, you'll understand why. *The Passion* is going to be bigger than Mel Gibson. It already is. For those of you who have never heard the story of who Jesus is, there will be a new appreciation and an awakening to the price paid by the Son of God over two thousand years ago. If movies have become the Bibles to our culture and movie theaters the pulpits of the world, you can see how potentially important Gibson's movie could be. Whether Hollywood likes it or not, *The Passion* has all the makings of a career milestone for Mel Gibson and a religious phenomenon for the rest of the world.

As you turn the pages of this book, reflect on the meaning of *The Passion* for your own life, because God is a very personal Father. Every day He gives us a new opportunity to live out the meaning of that Passion, and He showers purpose on our lives. I can't believe the journey God has brought me on from that day He tested my obedience and opened doors for me to meet with Mel Gibson. He has adventures in store for you too. May you walk in perpetual blessing.

Holly McClure

"HIS BLOOD BE ON US AND ON OUR CHILDREN!"
An Introduction

*M*y first crucifix, a gift from my aunt, was made of white plaster, about a foot long. I was rather young, and the novelty of it fascinated me; I had seen such images only from a distance. I examined it carefully, running my fingers over each detail of the wounds, nails, and thorns.

It was beautiful. But before long I concluded that it was much too clean. Pulling out my box of water-colors, I painted it, with bloody reds and purples dominating the whole. All in white, it seemed, the Figure had looked like a ghost. Now, with livid flesh, He looked at last like a Man, if a suffering One.

Since that time, the sacred image of Christ on the

Cross has met me and challenged me countless times in church, on the walls at home, and in the homes of friends. Like millions of Christians through the ages, after years of familiarity, I still find myself strangely drawn to the crucifix, to reflect on the agony portrayed there. And the images I find the most honest, I also find the most compelling: I mean the kind of dark, grisly crucifix so beloved in Latin culture, and so unsettling to our own.

Why unsettling? I once heard a religion teacher in a parochial school complain about the crucifix. She insisted that the sight of a dying Human Being on an instrument of torture simply shouldn't be tolerated in a school or even a church. Too negative, she said, too messy, too bloody, too disturbing. Think of the children!

I do think of the children. And when I do, I also think of the broken, bloody world they inhabit, the same world into which their Savior came as a Child, the same world that nailed Him to that Cross. I remember that they were born in blood, they may well die in blood, and in the meantime, they will no doubt see a great deal more of blood.

The question is not whether our children, and we ourselves, will be confronted with blood. Life itself is crimson-stained. The question is this: What kind of meaning will we find in the blood? Will we learn that "life is in the blood" (Leviticus 17:11)? Will we know that forgiveness, healing, and grace are in the blood? Or will we believe the lies of our time that blood is a mere commodity, cheap entertainment, or the never-quite-satisfied taste of revenge?

The crucifix has much to teach us about the true meaning of blood, if we will only pay attention. A great deal of traditional Christian prayer and meditation has been precisely the attempt to pay that kind of attention. Such prayer dwells on the passion of Jesus Christ as prophesied and foreshadowed in the Old Testament; preached and remembered in the four Gospels; interpreted and lived in the rest of the New Testament.

The Power of the Passion

The Passion is an immense thing, a supernatural and divine thing, and thus a dangerous thing. Understood, appreciated, and embraced for its own sake—genuinely, if never fully—it has the power to overthrow us and, overthrowing, to save us. Misunderstood, dismissed, or manipulated for a diabolical agenda, it still has the power to overthrow us and, overthrowing, to damn us.

The history of the Church provides ample illustrations of both kinds of encounter with the Passion. The Apostle Paul so deeply entered its depths that he bore on his body "the marks of Jesus" (Galatians 6:17). Yet he also wrote in tears of those he called "enemies of the cross of Christ" (Philippians 3:17)—Christians who confused and abused the message of Christ's suffering, death, and resurrection.

The horrible pogroms against Jews across the centuries display perhaps most starkly the hellish outcome when people attempt to harness the power of the Passion for selfish causes. Some Christians heard the sacred story and twisted it into a summons to vengeance against "the Christ killers," refusing to recognize that they had to include themselves in that wretched category. For them, the blood of Christ was not a costly and humbling invitation to goodness, but rather a convenient and explosive excuse for evil.

Nevertheless, there were men and women in every generation who hid themselves deeply in the precious wounds of Jesus and found there the bloody womb for a new birth. The Spanish Franciscan Maria (Coronel) of Agreda and the German Augustinian Anne Catherine Emmerich were two such Christians. Excerpts from Scripture and from the works of these two women form the basis for the forty reflections on Our Lord's passion presented here.

Maria of Agreda (1602–1665)

Maria Coronel entered the convent in Agreda, Castile, as a teenager, and took the name Maria de Jesus. By the age of twenty-five—over her protests—she was made abbess and, except for three years, remained the superior there for the rest of her life. During the time of her administration, the convent became one of the most fervent in all Spain, and she died with a reputation for great holiness. The cause for her canonization was introduced in 1762 by the Congregation of Rites at the request of the Court of Spain.

Maria is chiefly known, however, for writing a book entitled *The Mystical City of God: A Divine History of the Virgin Mother of God.* Though the text focuses on the life of Mary, her life is intimately intertwined with that of her Son. So the volume in part attempts to take us up close to the events of Our Lord's passion.

The Mystical City was first conceived nine years after Maria became a nun, but written down ten years later at the command of her confessor. She wrote the first part, consisting of four hundred pages, in only twenty days. Her desire was to keep it from publication, but a copy was sent to the Spanish King Philip IV. Later, in obedience to another confessor, she tossed the book and all her other writings into the flames. Then, in 1655, a third command of her spiritual director caused her to start again. She finished the project in 1670.

The Mystical City is presented as a record of special messages from God, received in contemplation and revealed in mysteries, that tell the life of

Mary. It overflows with elaborate detail, describing both interior and exterior events beginning with the Virgin's conception and extending to her coronation in heaven. As soon as the text found a public beyond Spain, it provoked a fierce storm of controversy.

It is not difficult to see why. Read as a precise theological treatise, a reliable historical account, an accurate scientific text, or even an exact record of what Maria heard and saw in her visions, the book presents numerous problems. She herself had been reluctant to see it published, perhaps sensing that the visions were intended more for her personal reflection than for public dissemination, and that much of what she saw and heard, as she often put it, was "indescribable" in the first place.

Difficulties were compounded by several factors: claims that Maria's confessors had tampered with the text; political tensions between France and Spain; theological debates between the Franciscans (her order) and their philosophical rivals; and certain mistranslations and misinterpretations of the original Spanish by non-native speakers. In general, the book was widely praised and approved in Spain, but condemned elsewhere.

Anne Catherine Emmerich (1774–1824)

Anne Catherine Emmerich entered the Augustinian convent at Agenetenberg, Dulmen, at the age of twenty-eight. Since childhood, the supernatural realm had seemed ordinary to her; she frequently experienced mystical visions and displayed extraordinary gifts. She predicted certain happenings accurately and could hear and see remote events. When the sick came to visit her, though she had no medical training, she could diagnose the causes of their problems and prescribe remedies that worked. Nevertheless, her own physical condition was frail and troublesome.

The sisters in the convent remained suspicious of her because of her unusual powers and poor health, and they were annoyed by her frequent ecstasies. In 1812 the government of Napoleon closed the institution, and Anne Catherine was forced to seek lodging with a poor widow. In 1813 she became bedridden.

Soon after, the stigmata—the wounds of Christ—appeared on her body, including the marks of the thorns. She tried to conceal them, as well as the crosses that appeared on her breast, but the word got out, and soon the local bishop sent a commission to examine the unusual phenomena. Though the examination was strict, in the end, the vicar general and three physicians who administered it were thoroughly convinced that the stigmata were genuine.

Some years later a noted German poet, Clemens Brentano (1778–1842), visited her, was converted, and remained daily at her bedside from 1820 to

1824, taking notes on her visions and mystical experiences as she described them. Each day he would
rewrite the notes, replacing her local dialect with
standard German, then read them back to her for her
revision and approval. Brentano was deeply
impressed by her purity, humility, and patience
under remarkably intense suffering.

In 1833, some years after the nun's death,
Brentano published the compilation of these notes,
under the title *The Dolorous Passion of Our Lord
Jesus Christ According to the Meditations of Anne
Catherine Emmerich*. The book focuses on her
visions of His suffering, death, and resurrection.
They are remarkable for their vivid detail, their
simplicity of style, and the passionate participation
of the visionary in the agonies described. We can't
be certain how much Brentano may have added in
his attempt to organize and clarify the material, but
the text reflects brightly the fire and purity of a soul
who was consumed by the passion of her Lord.
Anne Catherine was declared "Venerable" by the
Church in 2001.

The Value of the Visions

In drawing from the visions of Maria and Anne
Catherine, we must use discretion, recognizing that
their value is primarily spiritual. Though the authors
were by no means doctors of history, science, or

theology, they were most certainly doctors of the soul. Both women display a marvelous understanding of the inner workings of the human mind and heart, and the subtle influences of grace. In their visions, then, we see not only Jesus, Mary, and their contemporaries, but ourselves as well. Held up as mirrors, the texts invite us all to recognize our role in the passion of Christ, so that we will kneel in gratitude before our Savior, confess our sins, and call out to Him for forgiveness, healing, and strength.

At the same time, we should keep in mind what the Church teaches about the place of *private* revelations—messages individuals claim have come to them directly from God, beyond the deposit of *public* Revelation that came to the world in Christ. Even when the Church approves such a revelation as worthy of belief, it does not hold us obliged to give it the same assent of faith we would give to Scripture.

How much more so, then, should we refuse to treat the visions of Maria and Anne Catherine as if they were somehow infallible. In fact, it would be difficult to do so consistently: The details of the two visions sometimes seem to contradict each other.

Instead, it seems to me, we should view these writings as a kind of spiritual drama: The events described, though offered in reference to historical events, are presented through an angle of vision akin

to that of the poet, the playwright, or the film director, rather than the historian, the scientist, or the
theologian. We find here a fusion of realistic detail
and mystical imagery, such as we might encounter in
the best of visionary cinema.

The Passion of the Christ

I was not at all surprised, then, to read in several
news reports and commentaries that director Mel
Gibson's exquisite production, *The Passion of the
Christ,* was influenced, at least in part, by Maria and
Anne Catherine's writings. To interpret through film
the sketchy Gospel accounts of Our Lord's passion,
a number of details must be filled in and an overarching creative vision of the story must be crafted.
In developing these cinematic elements, it only
makes sense that Mr. Gibson, himself a devout
Christian, would mine the riches of two profound
Christian souls who spent so much of their lives at
the foot of the Cross.

Predictably, once the association of Mr. Gibson's
film with Maria and Anne Catherine was suggested
in public, the works of the two visionaries were scru-
tinized, in particular by the director's critics. Those
who were already convinced that the Gospel
accounts themselves are hopelessly anti-Semitic had
condemned the film for reflecting too closely, in their
estimation, the evangelists' perspective. By scouring

these women's visions as well for evidences of anti-Semitism, they hoped to strengthen their claims that Mr. Gibson's work was flawed.

Given the deeply rooted animus against Jews in the cultures of Spain and Germany, it would be miraculous indeed to find no traces of such sentiment in Maria's and Anne Catherine's writings. These two women were shaped in certain regrettable ways by the evils of their times, as are we all, to one degree or another. Nevertheless, the more telling aspect of their visions is their fervent, repeated insistence that *each one* of us—of every national and ethnic background, every religion, and every generation—is in some sense a "Christ killer"; we all bear the shame and the blame for deicide, the murder of God. In this light, any pogrom claiming to avenge His death would have to begin with suicide.

The Reason for This Book

No doubt the present work will receive some share of such accusations of anti-Semitism. After all, these reflections on Our Lord's passion are based on the Gospels and the writings of the visionaries, and I freely confess that I believe Mr. Gibson's film on the same subject to be a work of spiritual and artistic genius. Even so, any claim that I am anti-Semitic would be utterly unfounded.

Twice now I have wept uncontrollably as I

walked through the grounds of the death camp at Dachau, a sincere token of my overwhelming sorrow for the horrors perpetrated on the Jewish people for so many generations. I was raised in a home free of anti-Semitic absurdities, and I would certainly not stoop to them now. But to those who would charge me with insensitivity in this regard at the very least, I would reply briefly:

First, I categorically reject the charge that the Gospels are tainted with anti-Semitism, though countless bigots have certainly twisted their meaning in an attempt to justify anti-Semitic behavior.

Second, though anti-Semitic passages can be found in Maria's and Anne Catherine's writings, I have extracted and freely adapted portions of their works in a way that focuses attention on our universal responsibility for Christ's passion rather than that of the first-century participants in these events.

Finally, I have concluded with considerable sadness that self-serving agendas have blinded many to the beauty and truth in the film *The Passion of the Christ*. I suppose we should expect that those who make their living by finding as many cases as possible of fatal disease (whether physical or spiritual) will tend to sound the alarm every time a man clears his throat. Mr. Gibson is not sick. He is simply clearing his throat to bring attention to the only lasting cure for those who are indeed desperately ill.

Curse or Blessing?

The beauty and truth of that cinematic work find their source in the blood of the Savior so powerfully depicted. When the ancient people of God sought liberation from their oppressors and protection from the avenging angel, they splashed the blood of the Paschal lamb around their doors (Exodus 12:7). In the same way, we must splash the blood of the eternal Paschal Lamb, Jesus Christ, on our homes and our hearts if we would be free, if we would be saved. The Cross should hang before us on our walls where it can plant itself daily in our thoughts. And not only the Blood, but the Body, Soul, and Divinity of Our Lord as well, received gratefully from His altar, must be our frequent and welcome Guest.

One particular scriptural text referring to this Blood has provoked especially sharp controversy in the debate over the alleged anti-Semitism of the Gospels. In the Passion account of St. Matthew, when Jesus' trial reaches its terrible climax, we read: "So when Pilate saw that he was gaining nothing, but rather that a riot was beginning, he took water and washed his hands before the crowd, saying, 'I am innocent of this righteous man's blood; see to it yourselves.' And all the people answered, 'His blood be on us and on our children!'" (Matthew 27:24–25).

Tragically, many Christians over the centuries have interpreted those last words of the crowd as a curse uttered by Jesus' Jewish enemies on themselves and their descendants. Viewing the statement as an admission of guilt, some have considered it an invitation to revenge, both human and divine—with horrific results. Understandably, Jewish people have been loathe to hear the words repeated.

Why, then, have I taken these very words as the title of this book's introduction? Certainly not to give offense. Instead, I believe that they hold the key to reconciliation and salvation, if we can only read them with new eyes.

It is the blood of Jesus, after all, that "cleanses us from all sin" (1 John 1:7). The "new covenant" of forgiveness is in His blood (Luke 22:20). His blood brings freedom (Revelation 1:5), victory (Revelation 12:10), and eternal life (John 6:54). Through His blood we are redeemed (Ephesians 1:7), purified (Hebrews 13:12), made righteous (Romans 5:9), and reconciled to God and one another (Colossians 1:20).

Knowing all this, I think we should read the words of the crowd not as a curse, but as a blessing. In calling for Christ's blood to be upon them and their children, they were actually praying that all the graces of salvation be poured out on them.

This is not to say that the people who cried out knew what they were doing. No doubt they would not have deliberately cursed themselves, nor would they have understood these words as a prayer.

Perhaps this was their way of dismissing the possibility that the execution would have any significant consequences.

In any case, what they meant by the words is not nearly as important as what God may have been saying through them, even without their awareness. According to the Gospel of John, a similar thing had happened when Caiaphas, the high priest, had said about Jesus: "It is expedient for you that one man should die for the people" (John 11:50). The priest had meant that Jesus was a troublemaker whose death would keep the Romans from overreacting to the situation. But John explains that God, using Caiaphas without his knowledge, was prophesying through him that Jesus' death would redeem us all (verses 51–52).

In this light, we would all do well to echo those profound words with a sense of urgency: "His blood be on us, and on our children!" We already bear, every one of us, the guilt of that blood; let us pray, then, for its cleansing. This little book is offered with a sincere prayer that in its pages, you will encounter as never before the power of Our Lord's blood, the graces of His passion—and the love of the One who laid down His life for you.

Paul Thigpen

I.

The Agony in the Garden

1
Christ's Vision of the World's Sins

Jesus went with them to a place called Gethsemane, and He said to His disciples, "Sit here, while I go over there and pray." And taking with Him Peter and the two sons of Zebedee, He began to be troubled and full of grief. Then He said to them, "My soul is very sorrowful, even to death; remain here, and watch with Me." Then going a little farther, He fell on His face and prayed.

Matthew 26:36–39*

*T*hose who would ponder the passion of Our Lord must begin, as do the Stations of the Cross, in the Garden of Gethsemane. The physical torture He endured at the hands of His executioners began only after His arrest. But long before the whips had ever carved crosses in His back, Jesus' exquisite interior suffering began as He wrestled in prayer on the dark slopes of Mount Olivet. He was "sorrowful, even to death"; even then, before the thorns and the nails, the grief alone came close to killing Him.

What extraordinary burden could weigh Him down so low that hell itself seemed in sight? What massive weight could press Him so fiercely that blood burst through His skin? In part, Anne

Catherine Emmerich tells us, Jesus was crushed by horror at a hideous sight: the sins whose price He had to pay.

The holier the soul, the deeper the revulsion to evil. How, then, can we begin to fathom the consequences for the soul of a perfectly holy Man when the wretched gravity of an entire planet—the sin of a whole world—came crashing down upon Him?

When Jesus left His disciples, I saw a number of frightful figures surrounding Him in an ever-shrinking circle. His sorrow and anguish of soul continued to increase, and He was trembling all over when He entered a grotto to pray, like a way-worn traveler hurriedly seeking shelter from a sudden storm. But the awful visions pursued Him even there, becoming increasingly clear.

This small cavern appeared to contain the awesome picture of all the sins that had been or were to be committed from the fall of Adam to the end of the world, and of the punishment they deserved. Jesus fell on His face, overwhelmed with unspeakable sorrow, and all the sins of the world displayed themselves before Him, under countless forms and in all their real deformity. He took them all upon

Himself, and in His prayer offered His own Person, worthy of adoration, to the justice of His heavenly Father, in payment for so awful a debt.

But Satan, who was enthroned amid all these horrors, filled with diabolical joy at the sight of them, let loose his fury against Jesus. He displayed before the eyes of His soul increasingly awful visions, addressing His humanity in words such as these: "Do You take even *this* sin upon Yourself? Are You willing to bear its penalty? Are You prepared to satisfy for *all* these sins?"

And now a long ray of light, like a luminous path in the air, descended from heaven; it was a procession of angels who came up to Jesus and strengthened and reinvigorated Him. The remainder of the grotto was filled with frightful visions of our crimes. Jesus took them all upon Himself, but His heart, so worthy to be adored, so filled with the most perfect love for God and man, was flooded with anguish and overwhelmed beneath the weight of so many abominable crimes.

The Dolorous Passion

Thank You, my Savior, for bearing my sins and canceling the debt I could never have paid.

2
Satan's Accusations and Temptations

*Jesus, full of the Holy Spirit, returned from
the Jordan, and was led by the Spirit for forty
days in the wilderness, tempted by the Devil.
... And when the Devil had ended every
temptation, he departed from Him until an
opportune time.*

Luke 4:1–2, 13

*S*atan, defeated by Our Lord in the wilderness
before His public ministry began, had retreated
until an opportunity arose to engage Him again.
What better opportunity than the agonized hours in
Gethsemane? Jesus had just withstood the onslaught
of infinite divine grief in the presence of perpetual
human wickedness. Now the Devil raised a second
siege against Our Lord's soul. Could Jesus withstand
the accusations and temptations of an enemy who
had studied His every move for a lifetime?

Anne Catherine suggests that the Devil knew
the human heart all too well. He recognized that a
good man, precisely because of his goodness, is
more apt to second-guess himself, to view his own
actions with the kind of humility that questions his
own motives. So Satan took advantage of the dark
mental fog induced by Jesus' intense suffering. He

accused Him of hidden pride and selfishness, pointing out as evidence the kinds of behavior that would indeed have been questionable in a man who was not also God.

Our Lord would thus have been tempted, in His human nature, to the sin of despair. If the Devil could not induce Jesus to surrender His trust in God, perhaps he could seduce Him into losing confidence in Himself—His identity and mission. In this way Satan repeated, more loudly now, the subtle but damning implication of his earlier words to Our Lord in the wilderness: "*If* You are the Son of God ..." "Are You really who You think You are? Perhaps You have deceived Yourself."

The tactic failed in Gethsemane. But the enemy of our souls still employs a similar scheme with the rest of us: "*If* you really are a child of God, you wouldn't have done *that*." His strategy of despair often meets with stunning success.

When this huge mass of iniquities, like the waves of a fathomless ocean, had passed over Jesus' soul, Satan brought forward numerous temptations, as he had formerly done in the desert, even daring to adduce various accusations against Him. "And do You take all these things upon Yourself," he exclaimed,

"You who are not without stain Yourself?" Then he laid to the charge of our Lord, with hellish impudence, a host of imaginary crimes. He reproached Him with the faults of His disciples, the scandals they had caused, and the disturbances that He had occasioned in the world by giving up ancient customs.

He accused Jesus of having been the cause of the massacre of the Innocents, as well as of the sufferings of His parents in Egypt; of not having saved John the Baptist from death; of having brought disunion into families, protected men of despicable character, refused to cure various sick persons, injured the Gerasenes by permitting demons to make swine cast themselves into the sea; of having deserted His family and squandered the property of others. In short, Satan, in the hopes of causing Jesus to waver, suggested to Him every thought by which he would have tempted at the hour of death an ordinary mortal who might have performed all these actions without a superhuman intention. In this way, there was not an action out of which Satan did not contrive to frame some accusation.

The Dolorous Passion

When the enemy of my soul reproaches me,
Jesus, defend me with Your truth.

3
"Remove This Cup"

*Jesus withdrew from them about a stone's
throw, and knelt down and prayed, "Father,
if Thou art willing, remove this cup from Me;
nevertheless, not my will, but Thine be
done." And there appeared to Him an angel
from heaven, strengthening Him. And being
in an agony He prayed more earnestly; and
His sweat became like great drops of blood
falling down upon the ground.*

Luke 22:41–45

*N*ot long before this sorrowful night, Jesus
had declared to His apostles: "Now is My
soul troubled. And what shall I say? 'Father, save
Me from this hour'?" No, for this purpose I have
come to this hour" (John 12:27).

How startling it is, then, to hear His outcry in the
Garden: "Remove this cup from Me!" Is any prayer
of Our Lord more unsettling than this? Hearing it,
we are tempted to think that in this terrible moment,
Jesus lost His courage, faltered in His resolve,
shrank from His mission.

Yet Anne Catherine reminds us—as did the
ancient fathers of the Church in commenting on this
passage—that Jesus was not stumbling spiritually

when He spoke this prayer. Rather, He was displaying clear and stunning evidence of His full humanity.

To be sure, He did not sin: He never chose nor
even desired anything other than the Father's perfect
will. Even now, He fortified this anguished petition,
before and after, with firm declarations that He was
submitting Himself completely to the divine plan. But
in this dreadful hour, Jesus drank to the dregs that
utterly human terror, wrenching the gut, no doubt
familiar to every man or woman who has ever faced
the grisly prospect of prolonged, excruciating pain.

"Remove this cup" was thus the natural groan of
human flesh as it recoiled from the sight of its own
bloody holocaust—even as the human soul of Jesus
reached up to embrace the Father's will.

Jesus' anguish was so great that He trembled and
shuddered as He exclaimed: "Father, if it is possible,
let this chalice pass from Me!" But the next moment
He added: "Nevertheless, not My will but Yours be
done." His will and that of His Father were one, but
now that His love had ordained that He should be
left to all the weakness of His human nature, He
trembled at the prospect of death.

Angels came and showed Him, in a series of
visions, all the sufferings that He was to endure in

order to atone for sin; how great was the beauty of man, the image of God, before the Fall, and how that beauty was changed and obliterated when sin entered the world. They showed Him the satisfaction that He would have to offer to Divine Justice, and how it would consist of a degree of suffering in His soul and body that would gather together all the sufferings due to the sinful tendencies of all humanity, since the debt of the whole human race had to be paid by that humanity which alone was sinless—the humanity of the Son of God.

No tongue can describe what anguish and what horror overwhelmed the soul of Jesus at the sight of so terrible an atonement—His sufferings were so great, indeed, that a bloody sweat issued forth from all the pores of His sacred body. Our Redeemer, on Mount Olivet, was pleased to experience and overcome that violent repugnance of human nature to suffering and death which constitutes a portion of all sufferings.

The Dolorous Passion

Give me grace, Father, to drink whatever cup You have poured for me.

4
Christ's Vision of the Church's Trials

*Jesus answered them, "Take heed that no one
leads you astray. For many will come in My
name, saying, 'I am the Christ,' and they will
lead many astray. ... Then they will deliver
you up to tribulation, and put you to death;
and you will be hated by all nations for My
name's sake. And then many will fall away,
and betray one another, and hate one another.
And many false prophets will arise, and lead
many astray. And because wickedness is
multiplied, most men's love will grow cold."*

Matthew 24:4–5, 9–12

*J*ust how much of the future God the Father
allowed Jesus to see in His earthly life, we
cannot know for sure. In emptying Himself and
taking "the form of a servant" (Philippians 2:7), in
His human nature He had voluntarily limited His
knowledge of certain things. The Gospel tells us, for
example, that the day and hour of Our Lord's return
in glory was hidden from Him (Matthew 24:36).
Nevertheless, we are assured that He knew ahead of
time He would one day be "mocked and scourged
and crucified" (Matthew 20:19), and He knew as
well that the Church He established would follow in

the footsteps of His suffering (Matthew 5:10–12; 10:16–28; 16:24; 24:4–11).

In her vision, Anne Catherine elaborated on this foreknowledge of Our Lord, examining the kinds of temptations He might have endured as a result of it. As we have seen, she portrayed Satan taking advantage of Jesus' prophetic insight by focusing on the loathsome details of His impending personal doom. Yet to no avail. Christ weathered the diabolical tempest, with its screaming challenge: "Are You able to suffer these things?"

But now, because of Jesus' awareness of His Church's future trials, He faced more haunting questions: "If I suffer these things, what good will it do? Will this fallen race turn its back on My gift? Is it worth the price?"

"He Himself knew what was in man" (John 2:25). Our Lord had seen the pride and the envy; the hatred and the rage; and the lust for wealth, power, pleasure, and fame. He could offer deliverance from all this to those who would come to Him. But how many would come? And how many would stay?

A succession of new and terrifying visions were presented before Jesus' eyes, and that feeling of doubt and anxiety which someone on the point of making some great sacrifice always experiences, arose in the soul of Our Lord, as He asked himself the tremendous question: "And what good will result from this sacrifice?" Now He beheld all the future sufferings, combats, and wounds of His heavenly Spouse, the Church. In a word, He beheld the ingratitude of men.

The soul of Jesus beheld all the future sufferings of His apostles, disciples, and friends. After this He saw the primitive Church, numbering but few souls in her fold at first, and then in proportion as her numbers increased, disturbed by heresies and schisms breaking out among her children, who repeated the sin of Adam by pride and disobedience. He saw the tepidity, malice, and corruption of an infinite number of Christians, the lies and deceptions of proud teachers, all the sacrileges of wicked priests, the fatal consequences of each sin, and "desolating sacrilege" in the kingdom of God (Matthew 24:15), in the sanctuary of those ungrateful human beings whom He was about to redeem with His blood at the cost of unspeakable sufferings.

The Dolorous Passion

Give me grace, Jesus, to be always grateful
for all You have done for me.

5
Christ's Vision of a Scattered Flock

My people have been lost sheep; their shep-
herds have led them astray, turning them
away on the mountains; from mountain to hill
they have gone, they have forgotten their fold.
All who found them have devoured them, and
their enemies have said, "We are not guilty,
for they have sinned against the Lord, their
true habitation."

Jeremiah 50:6–7

*A*ttacking wolves can tear a shepherd's flesh.
But wayward sheep can cause an injury more
bitter still: They will break a shepherd's heart.

Our Lord, "the Good Shepherd," knew He must
lay down His life for the sheep (John 10:11). By His
death, He would gather them into "one flock" (v.
17). But in their willfulness they could still wander,
scatter, and lose their way in the search for greener
pastures, where predators would pick them off.

Anne Catherine told how Jesus' terrifying
visions continued as He watched His beloved flock
disperse in the centuries to come—following multitudes of "hirelings" who were themselves mis-
guided, chasing after the wind. And His heart was
pierced as He saw the wilderness devour so many of

those for whom He would give His life.

Jesus beheld all the apostates, heretical leaders, and pretended reformers, who deceive men by an appearance of holiness. They vied with each other in tearing the seamless robe of His Church. Many avoided His compassionate embrace and hurried on to the abyss where they were finally swallowed up.

In His agony Jesus saw countless numbers of other men who did not dare openly to deny Him, but who passed on in disgust at the sight of the wounds of His Church, just as the Levite had passed by the poor man who had fallen among robbers in the parable of the Good Samaritan. Like cowardly and faithless children, who desert their mother in the middle of the night at the sight of the thieves and robbers to whom their negligence or their malice has opened the door, they fled from His wounded spouse, the Church.

He beheld all these men, sometimes separated from the True Vine, and taking their rest amid the wild fruit trees, sometimes like lost sheep, left to the mercy of the wolves, led by base hirelings into bad pastures, and refusing to enter the fold of the Good Shepherd who gave His life for His sheep. They were wandering homeless in the desert in the midst of the sand blown about by the wind, and were obstinately determined not to see His city placed upon a hill, which could not be hidden, the house of His spouse, His Church built upon a rock, with which He had promised to remain to the end of ages. They built upon the sand wretched tenements, which they were continually pulling down and rebuilding, but in which there was neither altar nor sacrifice.

They had weathercocks on their roofs, and their doctrines changed with the wind. Consequently, they were forever in opposition one with the other. They never could come to a mutual understanding, and were forever unsettled, often destroying their own dwellings and hurling the fragments against the Cornerstone of the Church, which always remained unshaken.

Jesus beheld them all, He wept over them, and was pleased to suffer for all those who do not see Him and who will not carry their crosses after Him in His city built upon a hill—His Church founded upon a rock, to which He has given Himself in the Holy Eucharist, and against which the gates of Hell will never prevail.

The Dolorous Passion

Keep me safe, Good Shepherd, in Your fold, and never let me wander.

6
Christ's Joyful Vision of the Saints

These all died in faith, not having received what was promised, but having seen it and greeted it from afar. ... Therefore, since we are surrounded by so great a cloud of witnesses, let us also lay aside every weight, and sin which clings so closely, and let us run with perseverance the race that is set before us, looking to Jesus the pioneer and perfecter of our faith, who for the joy that was set before Him endured the cross, despising the shame, and is seated at the right hand of the throne of God.

Hebrews 11:13; 12:1–2

*I*n the midst of such overwhelming anguish over our sin and His suffering, was there not to be even a single, brief moment of relief for Our Lord? What thought, what hope could possibly be bright enough to shine in so deep a darkness and bring Him comfort?

The Devil had tried to torment Him with the sorrowful prospect of millions who would spurn or betray His love. But then, according to Anne Catherine, the Father's mercy burst through the blackness with a vision of millions more—this time, the men and women of all the ages who would give their hearts to Him in grateful love for His sacrifice. Our Lady and St. Joseph, Moses and Elijah, St. Francis, St. Catherine, St. Anthony, St. Thérèse—He would make it possible for all these and countless others to have a place at His side in glory for all eternity.

In that moment, Jesus caught a glimpse of His stunningly beautiful Bride, the Church (Revelation 19:6–9). He knew then that He would be willing to move heaven and earth in order to save and embrace Her. So "for the joy set before Him," He "endured the cross, despising the shame."

The abyss opened before Jesus, and He had a vision of that place where the faithful departed were dwelling. He saw Adam and Eve, the patriarchs, the prophets, and the righteous, the parents of his Mother, and John the Baptist, awaiting His arrival in the lower world with such intense longing, that the sight strengthened and gave fresh courage to His loving heart. His death was to open heaven to these captives; His death was to deliver them out of that prison in which they were languishing in eager hope!

When Jesus had, with deep emotion, looked upon these saints of antiquity, angels presented to Him all the bands of saints of future ages, who, joining their labors to the merits of His passion, were through Him to be united to His Heavenly Father. Most beautiful and consoling was this vision, in which He beheld salvation and sanctification flowing forth in ceaseless streams from the fountain of redemption opened by His death.

The apostles, disciples, virgins, and holy women; the martyrs, confessors, hermits, popes, and bishops; and large bands of religious of both sexes— in one word, the entire army of the blessed— appeared before him. All bore on their heads triumphal crowns. Their whole life, and all their actions, merits, and power, as well as all the glory of their triumph, came solely from their union with the merits of Jesus Christ.

The army of the future saints passed before the soul of our Lord, which was thus placed between the longing patriarchs and the triumphant band of the future blessed. And these two armies joining together, and completing one another, so to speak, surrounded the loving heart of our Savior, forming around it a crown of victory.

The Dolorous Passion

Precious Lord, let my devotion to You bring joy to Your heart.

7
Judas' Sins—and Ours

While [Jesus] was still speaking, Judas came, one of the twelve, and with him a great crowd with swords and clubs, from the chief priests and the elders of the people. Now the betrayer had given them a sign, saying, "The one I kiss is the man; seize Him. And he came up to Jesus at once and said, "Hail, Master!" And he kissed Him.

Matthew 26:47-49

*W*hat sting is as sharp as betrayal by a friend? And what insult is more bitter than betrayal through a kiss, the sweetest sign of friendship made poison? Worst of all, who could be so brazen, so wicked, so foolish as to betray with a kiss a friend who was the Son of God?

Who, indeed? Judas, yes—but also any one of us.

In her vision Maria explores the complex evil in Judas' heart, and in doing so, she shines the light of conviction on us all. The Gospel accounts only hint at the vices and weaknesses that could have led to so heinous a crime: Judas was dishonest (John 12:6), greedy (Matthew 26:14–16), hypocritical (Matthew 26:20–25), devious (Luke 22:4; John 18:2), audacious (Luke 22:48), and subject to diabolical impulses

(Luke 22:3; John 13:2). Maria's vision exposes this den of disorders in the traitor's heart, and when she identifies them, we realize—if we are honest—that such serpents may crawl through the crevices of our own souls as well.

So Judas betrayed his kindest friend, his most generous benefactor, the dear Son of God? Which of us has not? "All have sinned and fall short of the glory of God" (Romans 3:23). Our sins may not be as glaring as those of Judas, but the Master we betray by our sins is the same.

During these words and prayers of the Author of life, Judas came forward to give the signal he had agreed upon with his cohorts. The signal was the customary kiss of peace, but in this case it was feigned. By this sign they were to identify Jesus as the One they should single out and arrest immediately.

The unhappy disciple had taken these precautions, not only because of greed for the money and hatred for his Master, but also because of the fear that filled him. For he dreaded the inevitable encounter with Christ in the future if He were not put to death on this occasion. Such an outcome he feared more than the death of his soul, of the death of His divine Master, and to prevent it he hurried to complete his treachery and sought to see the Author of life die at the hands of His enemies.

The betrayer then ran up to his most humble Lord and, as the worst of hypocrites, hiding his hatred, he pressed on Jesus' face the kiss of peace. In this one act of treason he committed so many and such formidable sins, that it is impossible to fathom their depths. He was treacherous, murderous, sacrilegious, ungrateful, inhuman, disobedient, false, lying, and unequalled in hypocrisy. And all this was brought together in one and the same crime perpetrated against the person of God made man.

Lament with great sorrow the fact that Judas, in his malice and treachery, has many more followers than Christ. Many are the unfaithful, many the bad Catholics, many the hypocrites, who call themselves Christians but sell Him, hand Him over, and seek to crucify Him again.

The Mystical City of God

Lord Jesus, forgive me for the times when I have followed Judas instead of You.

8
The Healing of the Slave

And when those who were about [Jesus]
saw what would follow, they said, "Lord,
shall we strike with the sword?" And one of
them struck the slave of the high priest and
cut off his right ear. But Jesus said, "No
more of this!" And He touched his ear and
healed him.

Luke 22:49–51

Those who came to arrest Jesus in the garden no doubt had heard accounts of His miracles. Such demonstrations of His power had caused people to speculate that He was Elijah returned from heaven, or John the Baptist returned from the grave, or some other prophet, or even the promised Messiah (Matthew 16:13–16). Nevertheless, this armed mob apparently remained unconvinced that Jesus was anything more than an ordinary mortal. Otherwise, who would have dared to lay hands on Him?

Perhaps they had dismissed all the breathless testimonies as tall tales. If so, Our Lord gave them one last chance in the garden to witness a miracle for themselves—and to believe. After St. Peter sliced off a slave's ear, Jesus healed the man on the spot.

The slave was one of their own, so they knew he would not have conspired to deceive them. No sleight of hand on Jesus' part could fake the restoration of a severed limb. Even so, at least some of the armed men and their companions refused to believe. Undeterred by the miracle, they bound Christ and dragged Him away.

How did they make sense of what they saw in a way that allowed them to remain skeptical? Anne Catherine saw the mob admitting that supernatural forces were at work, but they labeled it sorcery. If it were the work of the Devil, they had all the more reason to arrest the man as dangerous.

By no means would it have been the first time that those who refused to believe in Jesus had justified their unbelief through contorted reasoning. When Our Lord had exorcised unclean spirits, some simply responded that "He casts out demons by the prince of demons" (Matthew 9:32–34). When God the Father had spoken from heaven to confirm His Son, "the crowd standing by heard," but some of them insisted it was only thunder (John 12:28–29). Then as now, there are those who fail to encounter God's power "because seeing they do not see, and hearing they do not hear" (Matthew 13:15).

The soldiers immediately surrounded Jesus, and the guards laid hands upon Him. Judas wanted to flee, but the Apostles would not allow it. They rushed at the soldiers and cried out, "Master, shall we strike with the sword?" Peter, who was more impetuous than the rest, seized the sword, and struck Malchus (John 18:10), the servant of the high priest, who wished to drive away the Apostles, and cut off his right ear. Malchus fell to the ground, and a great tumult ensued.

When Peter struck Malchus, Jesus said to him, "Put your sword back into its place; for all who take up the sword will perish by the sword." Then He said, "Let me cure this man." And approaching Malchus, He touched his ear, prayed, and it was healed.

But the soldiers who were standing near, as well as the guards and the six Pharisees, were far from being moved by this miracle. Instead, they continued to insult Our Lord, and said to the bystanders, "It's a trick of the Devil! The powers of witchcraft made the ear appear to be cut off, and now the same power gives it the appearance of being healed."

The Dolorous Passion

Lord, let me never be blind or deaf to Your power.

9
Jesus Goes Willingly to Die

Then Jesus said to [Peter] ... "Do you think that I cannot appeal to My Father, and He will at once send Me more than twelve legions of angels?" ... At that hour Jesus said to the crowds, "Have you come out as against a robber, with swords and clubs to capture Me? ... But all this has taken place, that the Scriptures of the prophets might be fulfilled."

Matthew 26:52–53, 55–56

More than once in His public ministry, Our Lord had walked unharmed through angry crowds seeking to kill Him. "His hour had not yet come" (John 7:30, 44; 10:39; 8:20, 59). But as the torch-bearing mob surrounded Him in Gethsemane, He knew the appointed time had arrived.

"When I was with you day after day in the temple," Jesus said to them, "you did not lay hands on Me. But this is your hour, and the power of darkness" (Luke 22:53).

Our Lord could have summoned all the hosts of heaven to defend Him. No doubt even at that moment they surrounded Him in the darkness, invisible in their glory, rank upon rank, sword in hand, ready to fight should He give the signal. Or He could have sent them away and done the deed Himself with only a word: At His command the universe had come into being, and at His command, it could dissolve into nothingness again (John 1:1–3).

But long before He had ever come to earth, God the Son had joined in perfect harmony with God the Father to will the world's salvation. For this reason He had been born, and for this reason He would die (John 18:37). Only a few hours before, He had gathered the apostles for the paschal feast, "knowing that the Father had given all things into His hands, and that He had come from God and was going to God" (John 13:3). The mission remained clear now, even as He met the enemy in the garden.

Together the Father and the Son had sent the Holy Spirit to inspire the prophets with a promise that the Savior would come. The Scriptures had declared it. Could God go back on His word? No— Jesus would fulfill the prophecy: "I have not turned backward. ... I have set My face like a flint" (Isaiah 50:5, 7).

In Maria's vision, on the day of Our Lord's betrayal, He spoke with His Father to review the providential plan. This season of prayer steeled Him for the horrendous combat to come.

Christ our Lord prayed: "My eternal Father, in obedience to Your will I gladly hasten on to satisfy Your justice by suffering even to death. In this way I will reconcile to You all the children of Adam, paying their debts and opening to them the gates of heaven that have been closed to them. I will seek those who have gone astray and lost their way, so that they may be restored by the power of My love.

"I will find and gather together the lost sheep of the house of Jacob (Isaiah 56:8), raise up the fallen, enrich the poor, refresh the thirsty, cast down the proud, and lift up the humble. I want to conquer hell and multiply the glories of the victory over Lucifer (1 John 3:8) and over the vices he has sown into the world. I want to raise up the banner of the Cross—beneath it, virtue, and all those who place themselves under its protection, will fight their battles."

The Mystical City of God

Beneath the royal standard of Your cross, Lord Jesus, I take my place for battle against the darkness.

II.

Our Lord on Trial

10
Christ's Enemies Gather

> *Now the chief priests and the whole council*
> *sought false testimony against Jesus that*
> *they might put Him to death, but they found*
> *none, though many false witnesses came*
> *forward.*
>
> Matthew 26:59–60

*J*esus once said, "I have not come to bring peace,
but a sword" (Matthew 10:34), and at no time
was that truth more clearly displayed than in the
hours of His passion. He was "a sign to be spoken
against" (Luke 2:34). Once He was arrested, those
He had offended gathered gleefully to speak against
this Sign from heaven who, simply by being true and
good, had proved them to be false and wicked.

When Anne Catherine read the souls of these
malcontents in her vision, she saw there a tangle of
bitter roots. Whatever their diverse motivations to
hatred, in one way or another each one had encoun-
tered Christ not as Savior, but as Stumbling Block
(1 Corinthians 1:23). Mingled among them were a
few disheartened friends of the Lord, along with
many more who had no excuse to hate Him, but little
courage to defend Him.

Observing all these troubled souls, the visionary

remarked simply and sadly: Things were the same then as they often are now.

The enemies of Jesus hurried to the tribunal of Caiaphas, escorted by the scribes and Pharisees of Jerusalem. They were accompanied by many of those merchants whom our Lord had driven out of the temple when they were holding market there. Also gathered were the proud religious teachers whom He had silenced before all the people—even some who had never been able to forgive the humiliation of being proved wrong when He had disputed with them in the temple at the age of twelve.

In addition was a large number of unrepentant sinners He had refused to cure; relapsed sinners whose diseases had returned; worldly young men He would not accept as disciples; greedy people He had enraged by causing the money they had been in hopes of possessing to be distributed in alms instead. Others were there who were disappointed because He had cured their friends—thus dashing their hopes of inheriting the property of those who had been close to death. There were people given to sensual indulgence, upset because He had converted their victims, and many despicable characters who made their fortunes by flattering and fostering the vices of powerful people. All these emissaries of Satan assembled in crowds round the palace of Caiaphas to bring forward all their false accusations.

While all these wicked creatures were busily consulting about what to do, anguish and anxiety filled the hearts of the friends of Jesus, for they were ignorant of the mystery about to be accomplished. They wandered around, sighing and listening to every different opinion. Each word they uttered gave rise to feelings of suspicion in those who heard them, and if they were silent instead, their silence was criticized.

Many well-meaning but weak and undecided individuals yielded to temptation, stumbled, and lost their faith. Indeed, the number of these who persevered was very small indeed.

Things were the same then as they often are now: People were willing to serve God if they met with no opposition from their fellows, but were ashamed of the Cross if held in contempt by others. The hearts of some, however, were touched by the patience displayed by our Lord in the midst of His sufferings, and they walked away silent and sad.

The Dolorous Passion

Lord, when Your truth obstructs the path of my desires, help me turn to the right road instead of stumbling over You.

11
Bearing His Reproach

*For it is for Thy sake that I have borne
reproach, that shame has covered my face. I
have become a stranger to my brethren, an
alien to my mother's sons. For zeal for Thy
house has consumed me, and the insults of
those who insult Thee have fallen on me.*

Psalm 69:7–9

*A*fter His arrest, in every place where Our
Lord was dragged and tormented, we hear
one long, ceaseless refrain: the taunts of those who
took pleasure in seeing Him humiliated. Insults and
indignities, sarcasm and slander, blasphemy and
mockery—a relentless chorus of abuse screeched
throughout the night, building to a crescendo of
outrage as He hung on the cross the next day.

More subtle, but still ruinous, were the ricochets of
these verbal missiles onto the friends of Christ. Anne
Catherine heard the malicious whispers of "respec-
table" people echoing in the streets of Jerusalem, as
tongues wagged and fingers pointed at those who had
followed Jesus. Anyone who ventured to speak on His
behalf was risking public denunciation and worse.

Two thousand years later, the tongues still wag;
those who defend Christ's truth often face open

derision or hidden character assassination. Their adversaries label them zealots, fanatics, extremists, bigots, troublemakers, and hypocrites for daring to affirm the demands of the gospel. Daily they are slandered by journalists, mocked by celebrities, and reviled by politicians.

Some are silenced by the opposition. But those who are willing to join Him "outside the camp" of respectability, "bearing abuse for Him" (Hebrews 13:13), can rejoice in His promise: "Everyone who acknowledges Me before men, I also will acknowledge before My Father who is in heaven" (Matthew 10:32).

As Jesus was led to trial, among the people a thousand different speculations were proposed and opinions given, such as these:

"Lazarus and his sisters will soon know who is this man in whom they have placed such firm reliance."

"Joanna, Chusa, Susannah, Mary the mother of Mark, and Salome will repent—but too late—the folly of their conduct."

"The partisans of this fanatical man, this inciter of rebellion, pretended to be filled with compassion for all who looked upon things in a different light from themselves. But now they won't know where to hide their heads. He will find no one now to cast garments and strew olive branches at His feet."

"Those hypocrites who pretended to be so much better than other people will get what they deserve, for they are all implicated with the Galilean."

"It is a much more serious business than was at first thought. I should like to know how Nicodemus and Joseph of Arimathea will get out of it. The high priests have mistrusted them for some time, for they made common cause with Lazarus. But they are extremely cunning. Even so, everything will now be brought to light."

Speeches such as these were uttered by persons who were exasperated, not only against the disciples of Jesus, but likewise with the holy women who had supplied His material needs. These women had publicly and fearlessly expressed their respect for His teachings and made known their belief in His divine mission.

But even though many spoke of Jesus and His followers in this contemptuous manner, yet there were others who held very different opinions. Of these some were frightened; others were overcome with sorrow. … But the number of those sufficiently daring to avow their admiration for Jesus openly was but small.

The Dolorous Passion

Jesus, dearest of friends, I will gladly bear with You the reproach of Your enemies.

12
The Lamb Led to Slaughter

He was oppressed, and He was afflicted, yet He opened not His mouth; like a lamb that is led to the slaughter, and like a sheep that before its shearers is dumb, so He opened not His mouth. By oppression and judgment He was taken away; and as for His generation, who considered that He was cut off out of the land of the living, stricken for the transgression of my people?

Isaiah 53:7–8

*P*erhaps the most riveting characteristic of both Anne Catherine's and Maria's visions is their vivid detail. Facial expressions, room furnishings, ambient noises, features of the landscape—nothing seems to escape their penetrating mystical senses. In such rich descriptions of what they saw and heard, we touch the very texture of these visions, feeling for ourselves a little something of what these women might have felt when such scenes first spread before them.

Always behind the sensual details, however, lie the overarching spiritual truths for whose sake the visions have been granted. Nowhere is this principle more clearly illustrated than in Anne Catherine's panorama of Jerusalem on the night Jesus was betrayed.

The torches of the mob have been ignited by the fires of rage in their hearts. Wretched and wandering the streets, pursued by demons, Judas becomes the Devil's icon of the impenitent soul stumbling toward damnation. A scarlet moon foreshadows the bloody orb that will herald the Last Judgment (Acts 2:20). And outside the city gates, the bleating lambs, penned for slaughter, chant of the Lamb of God, strangely silent as He approaches His own red holocaust.

I saw feelings of hatred and fury burst forth in different parts of the city, looking like fire. The flames traveled the streets, merged with other fires they met, and proceeded in the direction of Mount Zion. Every moment they blazed more fiercely, and at last they came to a stop beneath the tribunal of Caiphas. There they remained, forming together a perfect whirlwind of fire.

As the crowds gathered around, the noise and confusion continued to increase. Mingling with these discordant sounds could be heard the bellowing of the beasts that were tethered outside the walls of Jerusalem, and the plaintive bleating of the lambs.

There was something especially touching in the

bleating of these lambs, which were to be sacrificed on the following day in the temple: For the one Lamb who was about to be offered a willing sacrifice did not open His mouth, like a sheep in the hands of the butcher that does not resist, or a lamb that is silent before the shearer (Acts 8:32–35). This Lamb was the Lamb of God, the Lamb without spot, the true paschal Lamb—Jesus Christ Himself.

The sky looked dark, gloomy, and threatening. The moon was scarlet, and covered with livid spots. It appeared to be in dread of reaching its fullness, because its Creator was then to die.

Near the south gate I beheld the traitor, Judas Iscariot, wandering about alone, and a prey to the tortures of his guilty conscience. He feared even his own shadow and was followed by many devils who endeavored to turn his feelings of remorse into black despair. In fact, thousands of evil spirits were busying themselves everywhere, tempting men first to one sin and then to another. It appeared as if the gates of hell were flung open, and Satan was madly striving and exerting his whole energies to increase the heavy load of iniquities that the Lamb without spot had taken upon Himself.

The Dolorous Passion

Lamb of God, who takes away the sins of the world, have mercy on us.

13
The Interrogation by Annas

*First they led Him to Annas, for he was
the father-in-law of Caiaphas, who was high
priest that year. ... The high priest then questioned Jesus about His disciples and His
teaching.*

*Jesus answered him, "I have spoken
openly to the world; I have always taught in
the synagogues and in the temple, where all
Jews come together; I have said nothing
secretly. Why do you ask Me? Ask those who
have heard Me, what I said to them; they
know what I said."*

*When He had said this, one of the officers
standing by struck Jesus with his hand, saying,
"Is that how You answer the high priest?"*

*Jesus answered him, "If I have spoken
wrongly, bear witness to the wrong; but if I
have spoken rightly, why do you strike Me?"*
John 18:13, 19–23

The Gospel of John tells us that Jesus' first interrogation was by Annas, who demanded to know
what He had taught. Our Lord suggested that Annas
interrogate instead the people who had heard His
preaching. After all—witnesses were abundantly

available, and they would no doubt get right down to business by reporting first whichever of His statements had been most provocative.

Annas and his cohorts considered such a reply an insult, and they reacted accordingly. In Anne Catherine's vision, the hostile testimonies then began.

The irony, of course, is that all the witnesses she saw come forward reported accurately what Jesus had said and done. But they drew the wrong implications from His ministry, concluding that He was a charlatan, a fool, a blasphemer, a sinner, a tool of the Devil. The issue, then, was not whether Our Lord had taught these things, or even whether He had stirred up trouble by saying them. He had indeed. The issue, rather, was whether what He had said was true, and what He had done was right.

The problem was this: If Jesus had in fact been sent by God, as He claimed, then Annas and his allies were in desperate trouble. That was a possibility they refused to entertain.

No wonder, then, that when the interrogators called for Jesus to respond to His accusers, He was silent. What could He say to those whose minds were closed and whose hearts were hardened?

Turning to the witnesses, Annas summoned them to bring forward their accusations. They all began to speak at once.

"He has called Himself king. He says that God is His Father, and that the Pharisees are an adulterous generation. He causes insurrection among the people. He cures the sick through the Devil's help on the Sabbath day.

"The people gathered around Him a short time ago and addressed Him by the titles of 'Savior' and 'Prophet.' He lets Himself be called the Son of God. He says He is sent by God.

"He predicts the destruction of Jerusalem. He doesn't fast; He eats with sinners, with pagans, and with tax collectors. He associates with prostitutes.

"Not long ago He said to someone who gave Him some water to drink that He could give the waters of eternal life. Anyone who drinks those living waters, He claimed, would never thirst again."

These accusations were all voiced at once. Some of the witnesses stood before Jesus and insulted Him with derisive gestures as they spoke. The armed men even went so far as to strike Him as they taunted Him: "Speak! Why don't You answer?"

The Dolorous Passion

Lord Jesus, when my mind is closed,
open it to Your truth.

14
Jesus Models the Beatitudes

*Then they seized Him and led Him away,
bringing Him into the high priest's house. ...
Now the men who were holding Jesus
mocked Him and beat Him; they also blind-
folded Him and asked Him, "Prophesy! Who
is it that struck You?" And they spoke many
other words against Him, reviling Him.*

Luke 22:54, 63–65

The physical abuse of Our Lord began in earnest
once He was brought to the house of the high
priest. Perhaps some of those present in the crowd
had heard Him preach the Beatitudes: "Blessed are
the meek. ..." Perhaps they had scoffed, protesting
that such ideals—humility, mercy, purity, poverty,
peace, justice—were only for the weak. If so, His
attitude and behavior this night should have given
them reason to pause, reconsider, and marvel.

Our Lord was clearly not weak, either in will or
in body. He had not fled from arrest, though He
knew what horrors lay head. He had shown
startling serenity and self-control under their
relentless interrogation. He did not crumble under
the violence of His tormenters. After enduring
hours of brutality without sleep, He was still strong

enough the next day to carry His cross.

Throughout this stunning display of strength, Maria observed in her vision, Jesus modeled perfectly the beauties of humility, mercy, and all the rest. When His followers were later called upon to do the same, they knew it could be done. He had led the way by example (1 Peter 2:20–23).

Throughout these injuries and tortures, and the ones that followed soon after, Jesus provided a firm foundation for the Beatitudes, those promises He had made earlier in His preaching. He gazed upon the poor in spirit, who were to imitate Him in this virtue, and said, "Blessed are You in being stripped of earthly goods; for by My passion and death I will bequeath you the kingdom of heaven as a secure and certain possession of voluntary poverty.

"Blessed are the meek who suffer and endure afflictions and trials. In addition to the joy of having imitated Me, they will inherit the earth of the hearts and the good will of men through the peacefulness of their dealings with others and the sweetness of their virtues.

"Blessed are those who weep while they sow in tears. As a harvest, they will receive the bread of understanding and life, and afterward the fruits of eternal joy and happiness.

"Blessed also are those who hunger and thirst for righteousness and truth. I will earn for them a satisfaction far beyond all their greatest desires, both in the kingdom of grace and in the kingdom of glory.

"Blessed are those who, imitating Me in My offers of forgiveness and friendship, in mercy have pity on those who injure and persecute them. I promise them the fullness of mercy from My Father.

"Blessed are the pure of heart, who follow Me in crucifying the flesh so they can maintain the purity of their souls. I promise them that by becoming like Me and participating in Me, they will gain the vision of peace and of My Divine nature.

"Blessed are the peaceful. By yielding their rights, they refuse to resist the evil-minded and deal with them instead with a sincere and peaceful heart without vengeance. They will be called My children, because they are imitators of my eternal Father. I will write them in My memory and in My mind as my adopted sons.

"Those who suffer persecution for righteousness' sake will be blessed heirs of My heavenly kingdom, since they suffer with Me."

The Mystical City of God

Jesus, teach me to imitate Your blessedness in adversity.

15
St. Peter's Denial

Peter followed at a distance; and when they had kindled a fire in the middle of the courtyard and sat down together, Peter sat among them. Then a maid, seeing him as he sat in the light and gazing at him, said, "This man also was with Him." But he denied it, saying, "Woman, I do not know Him."

And a little later someone else saw him and said, "You also are one of them." But Peter said, "Man, I am not." And after an interval of about an hour still another insisted, saying, "Certainly this man also was with Him; for he is a Galilean." But Peter said, "Man, I do not know what you are saying." And immediately, while he was still speaking, the cock crowed.

And the Lord turned and looked at Peter. And Peter remembered the word of the Lord, how He had said to him, "Before the cock crows today, you will deny me three times." And he went out and wept bitterly.

Luke 22:54–62

*A*fter the account of Judas' betrayal, the story of St. Peter's denial is perhaps the most bitter episode recorded in the Gospels. In some ways, in fact, Peter's actions are even more difficult for us to swallow, for they seem more out of character than those of Judas.

The Gospel writers tell us that Judas was a thief, had a love for silver, and had plotted to sell out his Friend (John 12:4–6; Matthew 26:14–16). Peter, on the other hand, had seemed so careless of danger as he walked on the stormy sea (Matthew 14:22–33), so fiercely and self-confidently loyal to Jesus (Matthew 26:33–35), so ready to call down fire from heaven to avenge Our Lord's honor (Luke 9:51–56), or to draw the sword in His defense (John 18:10–12).

Nevertheless, "Jesus did not trust Himself to them, because He knew all men" (John 2:24–25). Our Lord prophesied both Judas' and Peter's terrible acts. He knew them both better than they knew themselves.

Anne Catherine reminds us that any one of us might, under similar difficult conditions, give in to fear and confusion to deny Our Lord. We never know ourselves completely; and so we must heed Jesus' warning to "watch and pray."

The cock then crowed again, and Jesus, who at that moment was led across the court, cast a look of mingled compassion and grief upon His apostle. This look of our Lord pierced Peter to the very heart.

He had forgotten all his promises and protestations to Our Lord, that he would die rather than deny Him. He had forgotten the warning given to him by Jesus. But when Christ looked at him, he felt the enormity of his fault, and his heart was nearly bursting with grief. He had denied his Lord, when that beloved Master was outraged, insulted, delivered up into the hands of unjust judges; when He was suffering all in patience and in silence.

What man will dare assert that he would have shown more courage than Peter with his quick and passionate temperament, if he were exposed to such danger, trouble, and sorrow—at a moment, too, when completely unnerved between fear and grief, and exhausted by the sufferings of this sad night? Our Lord left Peter to his own strength, and he was weak, as are all who forget the words: "Watch and pray, that you may not enter into temptation" (Matthew 26:41).

The Dolorous Passion

I don't know what lies in the depths of my own heart, Lord; I can only trust myself to Your grace.

16
Unseen Realities

The high priest stood up and said, "Have You no answer to make? What is it that these men testify against You?" But Jesus was silent. And the high priest said to Him, "I adjure You by the living God, tell us if You are the Christ, the Son of God."

Jesus said to him, "You have said so. But I tell you, hereafter you will see the Son of Man seated at the right hand of Power, and coming on the clouds of heaven."

Matthew 26:62–64

To the angry mob who watched as Jesus was interrogated in Caiaphas' house, He seemed utterly alone, abandoned, a speck of human debris about to be swept away before a whirlwind of powerful men and their lusts and whims. But all these were blind. In truth, as Anne Catherine saw in her vision, Jesus was the only one present with any genuine power—the strength of holiness, made perfect in weakness (2 Corinthians 12:9). The rest were puppets of dark forces who would soon tire of them, toss them away, and find new play toys.

The visionary knew that the images of the spiritual realm she beheld in this scene were symbolic:

"These things," she observed, "are always shown to me under the appearance of some material object, which renders them less difficult to comprehend and impresses them in a more clear and forcible manner on my mind." Nevertheless, she also recognized that the realities they symbolized were far more substantial than what usually passes for reality in our daily lives. In our response to these unseen forces, both good and evil, we too are choosing one road or another to eternity.

"Hereafter you shall see the Son of Man sitting on the right hand of the power of God, and coming in the clouds of heaven." While Jesus was pronouncing these words, a bright light appeared to me to surround Him. Heaven was opened above His head; I saw the Eternal Father. But no words from a human pen can describe the direct perception of Him that was then entrusted to me. I likewise saw the angels, and the prayers of the righteous ascending to the throne of God.

At the same moment I perceived the yawning abyss of hell like a fiery meteor at the feet of Caiaphas. It was filled with horrible devils; only a thin gauze separated him from its dark flames. I could see the diabolical fury with which his heart was overflowing, and the whole house looked to me like hell.

At the moment that Our Lord pronounced the solemn words, hell appeared to be shaken from one end to the other and then, as it were, to burst forth and flood every person in the house of Caiaphas with feelings of redoubled hatred towards Our Lord. The despair and fury that Jesus' words produced in hell were shown to me under the appearance of a thousand terrifying figures in different places. I remember seeing, among other frightful things, a number of little black objects, like dogs with claws, that walked on their hind legs.

I saw these horrible phantoms enter into the bodies of most of the bystanders, or else climb atop their heads or shoulders. And I saw in the neighborhood of the temple many other apparitions, which resembled prisoners loaded with chains. All whose hearts were not utterly corrupted felt extremely terrified at these events, but those who were hardened were aware of nothing but a growing hatred and anger against Our Lord.

The Dolorous Passion

Save me, Lord, from the powers of darkness, and keep me in Your marvelous light.

17
His Hour Had Come

Then turning to the disciples [Jesus] said privately, "Blessed are the eyes which see what you see! For I tell you that many prophets and kings desired to see what you see, and did not see it, and to hear what you hear, and did not hear it. ... I have a baptism to be baptized with; and how I am constrained until it is accomplished!"

Luke 10:23–24; 12:50

*I*n the course of such relentless torments, even a few moments of relief for Jesus would have been a priceless gift from the Father. Anne Catherine saw in her vision just such a reprieve, however brief.

She watched as Our Lord was left alone by His torturers in a wretched, filthy dungeon cell with a single sliver of a hole for air, opening to the sky. The morning had just broken. A solitary sunbeam, pale but piercing the darkness, descended from heaven on His broken body, a ray from His Father's face.

To her amazement, Jesus did not cry out to Him in agony. Instead, He lifted up His chains and gave Him thanks. The mystery of the ages was unfolding.

Prophets had sung of this day. Angels had longed to behold it (1 Peter 1:10–12). For this very time He had been born; all the moments of His life now converged in this moment. This day was the pivot on which all human history turned, the epicenter of an upheaval that would overthrow the world.

His hour had come.

Jesus continued to pray for His enemies and they, being at last tired out, left Him in peace for a short time. He leaned against the pillar to rest, and a bright light shone around Him. The day was beginning to dawn—the day of His passion, the day of our redemption.

A faint ray penetrating the narrow vent hole of the prison fell upon the holy and immaculate Lamb, who had taken upon Himself the sins of the world. Jesus turned toward the ray of light, raised His fettered hands, and in the most touching manner gave thanks to His heavenly Father for the dawn of that day, which had been so long desired by the prophets (Matthew 13:17; Luke 10:24). For this day He Himself had so ardently sighed from the moment of His birth on earth, and concerning it He had said to His disciples, "I have a baptism to be baptized with; and how I am constrained until it is accomplished!" (Luke 12:50).

I prayed with Him; but I cannot recall the words

of His prayer, for I was so completely overcome and touched to hear Him give thanks to His Father for the terrible sufferings He had already endured for me—and for the still greater pains He was about to endure. I could only repeat over and over with the greatest fervor, "Lord, I beg You, give me these sufferings. They belong to me. I have deserved them in punishment for my sins."

I was quite overwhelmed with feelings of love and compassion when I looked upon Him thus welcoming the dawn of the great day of His sacrifice. The ray of light that penetrated into His prison might, indeed, be compared to the visit of a judge who wishes to be reconciled to a criminal before the sentence of death he has pronounced upon him is executed.

The Dolorous Passion

Father, give me grace to be grateful for the unfolding of Your plan in my life—even when it remains to me a mystery.

18
Judas Despairs

When Judas, His betrayer, saw that [Jesus] was condemned, he repented and brought back the thirty pieces of silver to the chief priests and the elders, saying, "I have sinned in betraying innocent blood."

They said, "What is that to us? See to it yourself." And throwing down the pieces of silver in the temple, he departed; and he went and hanged himself.

Matthew 27:3–5

The Devil knows how to quote Scripture and twist it for his own purposes; he used the strategy during Christ's forty days in the wilderness. Trying to seduce Jesus into jumping off the pinnacle of the temple, the adversary slyly cited a biblical psalm out of context (Luke 4:9–11; Psalm 91:11–12). But Our Lord saw through the ruse and sent the Devil on his way.

In Anne Catherine's vision, Satan used the same strategy with Judas—but this time, Satan won.

Judas had come to feel regret for his crime, perhaps even remorse. For that very reason, the enemy of his soul could no longer dangle silver or any other bait before his eyes. Instead, the new diabolical tactic was to intensify the traitor's self-loathing—and thus to steal his hope.

St. Peter, like Judas, sinned despicably against his Lord. But Peter, having repented, threw himself on the mercy of the Judge. Judas chose instead to appoint himself executioner.

I beheld Judas rushing back and forth like a madman in the valley of Hinnom. Satan was by his side in a hideous form, trying to drive him to despair. The demon whispered in his ear all the curses that the prophets had hurled upon this valley, where the people had once sacrificed their children to idols (2 Chronicles 28:3; 33:6). It seemed as if all these maledictions were directed personally against him, as Satan quoted them: "They shall go forth and look on the dead bodies of the men that have rebelled against me; for their worm shall not die, their fire shall not be quenched" (Isaiah 66:24).

Then the Devil murmured in Judas' ears, "Cain, where is your brother Abel? What have you done? His blood cries to me for vengeance. You are cursed upon earth, a fugitive forever" (Genesis 4:9–12).

When Judas reached the brook of Kidron and saw the Mount of Olives, where he had betrayed Jesus, he shuddered and turned away. Again the words of Our

Lord vibrated in his ear, "Friend, why are you here? Judas, do you betray the Son of Man with a kiss?" (John 18:1–3; Matthew 26:50; Luke 22:48).

Horror filled the traitor's soul, his head began to swim, and the archfiend again whispered, "It was here that David crossed the Kidron when he fled from Absalom. And Absalom put an end to his life by hanging himself" (2 Samuel 18:9–15).

Overcome by these terrible thoughts, Judas rushed on and reached the foot of the mountain. It was a dreary, desolate spot filled with rubbish and putrid remains. Discordant sounds from the city reverberated in his ears, and Satan continually repeated: "They are now about to put Him to death. You have sold him. Don't you know the words of the law: 'Whoever sells a soul among his brethren, and receives the price of it, must die' (Deuteronomy 24:7)? Put an end to your misery, wretched man; put an end to your misery!"

Overcome by despair, Judas tore off his belt and hanged himself on a tree that grew in a crevice of the rock.

The Dolorous Passion

Jesus, when despair threatens to overwhelm me,
renew my hope in Your mercy.

19
A Parody of Palm Sunday

Throwing their garments on the colt they set
Jesus upon it. And as He rode along, they
spread their garments on the road. As He
was now drawing near, at the descent of the
Mount of Olives, the whole multitude of the
disciples began to rejoice and praise God
with a loud voice for all the mighty works
that they had seen, saying, "Blessed is the
King who comes in the name of the Lord!"

Luke 19:35–38

*O*nly a few days before, Jerusalem had over-
flowed with crowds who praised Jesus as
David's royal Son, refusing to be silenced. They had
adorned the streets before Him with their coats and
palm branches, eager to see Him, catch His eye, and
touch Him. For one fleeting, glorious moment, the
people recognized Him, proclaimed the truth about
Him, and embraced Him.

According to Anne Catherine, on the way to
Pilate's palace that boisterous scene was repeated—
but this time as a diabolical parody. Once again the
crowd could not be restrained, but now they shouted
insults. The pavement was littered once more, but
with debris to make Him stumble. The mob was again

eager to see Him—but this time, so they could exult in His degradation. They hoped to catch His eye—now, so they could mock Him. And they delighted in touching Him, but this time with cruel blows.

Thus they proved the old saying: The Devil is God's ape, stupidly mimicking His actions. He cannot create; He can only pervert what God has made. So his works are a grotesque travesty, like exaggerated paint on the face of an aging harlot on stage.

The greatest humiliation in Satan's burlesque of Palm Sunday did not belong, then, to Christ. As would soon become clear, the Devil had shown himself to be Heaven's buffoon.

The malicious enemies of our Savior led Him through the most public part of the town to take Him before Pilate. Caiaphas, Annas, and many others of the chief council walked first in festival attire. They were followed by a multitude of scribes and many others, among whom were the false witnesses and the wicked Pharisees who had taken the most promi-nent part in accusing Jesus. Our Lord followed at a short distance, surrounded by soldiers and led by armed men.

The multitude thronged on all sides and followed the procession, thundering forth the most fearful oaths and curses, while groups of people were hurrying back and forth, jostling one another. Jesus was stripped of all His clothes except His undergarment, which was stained and soiled by the filth that had been flung on it. A long chain was hanging around His neck, and it struck His knees as He walked.

His hands were shackled, and the armed men dragged Him by the ropes fastened around his waist. He staggered rather than walked. He was almost unrecognizable from the effects of His sufferings during the night. He was pale and haggard, His face swollen and bleeding, and each moment His merciless persecutors increasingly tormented Him.

They had gathered together a large body of the dregs of the people in order to make this disgraceful entrance into the city a parody of His triumphal entrance on Palm Sunday. They mocked Him, and with derisive gestures they called Him king. They tossed in His path stones, bits of wood, and filthy rags. They made a game of it, and by a thousand taunting speeches they mocked Him during this pretended triumphal entry.

The Dolorous Passion

Jesus, I should reflect Your image, but my sins make me a parody of You; cleanse me, so that I might sincerely imitate You.

20
The Enigma of Pilate

*As soon as it was morning the chief priests,
with the elders and scribes, and the whole
council held a consultation; and they bound
Jesus and led Him away and delivered Him
to Pilate. And Pilate asked Him, "Are you
the King of the Jews?" And He answered
him, "You have said so." And the chief
priests accused Him of many things. And
Pilate again asked Him, "Have You no
answer to make? See how many charges they
bring against You." But Jesus made no
further answer, so that Pilate wondered.*

Mark 15:1–5

*P*ontius Pilate presents us with an enigma. In
the Gospel accounts he is one moment hostile
to Jesus' enemies, and the next, annoyed with Jesus
Himself. He boasts of his power, but seems to think
it fragile nonetheless. He insists that Christ is innocent, but in the end, condemns Him to death.

Tossed by indecision, the Roman governor
dashes in and out of the praetorium between the
Accused and the accusers—asking worried questions, debating doctrines of an alien religion he
despises, looking for someone to relieve him of the

troublesome decision he faces. Through it all, above all, Pilate is driven by fear: of the local religious leaders, of the mob, of his wife's disturbing dreams, and most especially of Jesus Himself.

As with other figures in the story, Anne Catherine's vision took her into the labyrinths of the Roman governor's mind. There she found a chaos of vices and passions, ignorance and confusion. It would be all too easy to write him off as a pathetic character; but if we are honest, we always glimpse in these interior scenes a reflection of our own miserable plight apart from the workings of grace.

The character of Pilate was debauched and undecided, but his worst qualities were an extreme pride and meanness that made him never hesitate in the performance of an unjust action, provided it answered his ends. He was excessively superstitious, and when in any difficulty had recourse to charms and spells. He was much puzzled and alarmed about the trial of Jesus; and I saw him running backward and forward, offering incense first to one god and then to another, and imploring them to assist him.

But Satan filled his imagination with still greater confusion. He first instilled one false idea and then another into his mind. His mind remained enveloped in darkness, and he became more and more undecided.

Pilate at first thought that he would acquit our Savior, whom he well knew to be innocent. But then he feared incurring the wrath of his false gods if he spared Jesus, as he fancied that He might be some kind of inferior deity, and thus obnoxious to them. He wondered: "Perhaps He is a secret enemy both of our gods and of the emperor. It might be most imprudent for me to spare His life. Who knows—maybe His death would be a triumph for my gods!"

Then he remembered the amazing dreams described to him by his wife, who had never seen Jesus. Again he changed his mind, and decided that it would be safer not to condemn Him. He tried to persuade himself that he wished to pass a just sentence. But he only deceived himself, for when he asked, "What is the truth?" he did not wait for the answer. His mind was filled with confusion, and he was quite at a loss how to act, as his sole desire was to entail no risk upon himself.

The Dolorous Passion

Lord, when I sink into confusion, let Your light and truth guide me.

21
Christ Before Herod

When [Pilate] learned that [Jesus] belonged to Herod's jurisdiction, he sent Him over to Herod, who was himself in Jerusalem at that time. When Herod saw Jesus, he was very glad, for he had long desired to see Him, because he had heard about Him, and he was hoping to see some sign done by Him. So he questioned Him at some length; but He made no answer. The chief priests and the scribes stood by, vehemently accusing Him. And Herod with his soldiers treated Him with contempt and mocked Him; then, arraying Him in gorgeous apparel, he sent Him back to Pilate.

Luke 23:7–11

*I*f we compare Herod and Pilate in the Gospel accounts, Herod comes across as the simpler man, and certainly the more shallow of the two. Pilate's inner turbulence runs deep: He recognizes his dilemma and agonizes over it. He asks the penetrating question, "What is truth?" (John 18:38). Herod, on the other hand, seems more childish. He is driven by curiosity; he wants to be entertained; he takes pleasure in mocking and bullying.

In Anne Catherine's vision, the king's interrogation sounds much like a modern tabloid reporter trying to interview a reluctant celebrity. Herod seems less interested in pursuing the truth than in enjoying a sensational story, or better yet, an exposé.

If that was the case, no wonder Our Lord had earlier warned His followers to "beware of the leaven of the Pharisees and the leaven of Herod" (Mark 8:15), using "leaven" as an image for hypocrisy (Luke 12:1). Herod, like the Pharisees on that occasion, was "seeking from Him a sign from heaven, to test Him" (verse 11). But the test was a sham, their minds were already made up—so Jesus understandably refused to play their morbid game.

Herod's curiosity had been stirred by the exalted language John the Baptist had used to announce Jesus' coming. He had also heard much about Him through his spy network. Though he asked a thousand questions, Jesus said nothing and stood before him with His eyes cast down.

"I have heard so much about Your wisdom and the religion You teach. Let me hear You answer and confound Your enemies. Are You the king of the Jews? Are You the Son of God? Who are You?

"You are said to have performed amazing

miracles. Work one now while I'm watching. Is it true that You have restored sight to the blind, raised up Lazarus from the dead, and fed two or three thousand people with a few loaves? Why don't You answer? Come on—work a miracle right now in front of me!"

Jesus still kept silence, and Herod's questions continued to gush out. "Who are You?" he demanded. "Where do You get Your power? How is it that You no longer possess it?

"Are You the one whose birth was foretold in such an amazing way? Kings from the East came to my father to see a newborn king of the Jews. Is it true that You were that Child? Did You escape when so many children were massacred? How did You manage to escape?

"Why have You been unknown for so many years? Answer my questions! Are You a king? Your appearance certainly isn't regal. I've been told that You were brought to the temple in triumph just a few days ago. What was the meaning of such a parade? Speak out at once! Answer me!"

Herod continued to question Jesus rapidly. But our Lord did not trust him with a reply.

The Dolorous Passion

Jesus, cleanse me of the leaven of hypocrisy.

22
The Scourging at the Pillar

Then Pilate took Jesus and scourged Him.
And the soldiers plaited a crown of thorns,
and put it on His head, and arrayed Him in a
purple robe; they came up to Him, saying,
"Hail, King of the Jews!" and struck Him
with their hands. Pilate went out again, and
said to them, "See, I am bringing Him out to
you, that you may know that I find no crime
in Him." So Jesus came out, wearing the
crown of thorns and the purple robe. Pilate
said to them, "Behold the man!" When the
chief priests and the officers saw Him, they
cried out, "Crucify Him, crucify Him!"

John 19:1–6

Scourging is no longer a legal punishment in our society, so we may have little appreciation of the horrors it involves. Many today are surprised to know that in the past, floggings were often so brutal as to be fatal. When the leather was sufficiently hardened, the blows savagely applied, and knots or even bits of jagged metal added to the tips, the scourge could tear the flesh from the bone. When the most sensitive body parts were targeted—face, palms, soles of the feet, genitals—the pain was excruciating.

And if enough blows were given, the loss of blood alone could lead to death.

Ironically, it seems that Pilate's intention in having Jesus scourged was actually to save His life. He thought the grisly sight would be enough to slake the mob's thirst for blood, and they would drop their demands for Christ's death. Even so, it was not to be. The scourging became instead the prelude to a savagery more brutal still when the crowd shouted, "Crucify Him!"

Maria's vision takes us close up to this gruesome scene. Though we may find it revolting, the sight can draw us more deeply—if we let it—into a startling mystery: "With His stripes, we are healed" (Isaiah 53:5).

So the Lord stood naked before a great crowd, and the six torturers bound Him cruelly to one of the pillars so they could scourge Him more easily. Then two at a time, they took turns flogging Him with the kind of inhuman brutality that is possible only in those possessed by Lucifer. The first two men scourged the innocent Savior with hard, thick cords, filled with rough knots.

In their blasphemous rage they strained all their physical powers to strike the blows. This first flogging raised in the flesh of the Son of God great welts and discolored swellings, so that the sacred blood pooled beneath His skin and disfigured His whole body. Right away the blood began to seep through the wounds.

Eventually the first two men stopped, and the second two took over the task—even more violently, as if they were in competition with the first two. They aimed their blows, with hardened leather straps, on the spots that were already hurting, causing the discolored swellings to burst open and spurt out the sacred blood until it spattered and even drenched the clothing of the torturers. It also trickled down in streams to the pavement.

These two men were then replaced by the third pair of scourgers. They began flogging the Lord with extremely tough rawhide strips, dried hard like willow twigs. They beat Him all the more savagely because they were slicing into the wounds already made by the previous flogging. In addition, they had been secretly incited to a more intense rage by the demons, who were filled with new fury at Christ's patience.

The Mystical City of God

Lamb of God, by the costly wounds You sustained, save us and heal us.

23
"Who Do You Say That I Am?"

Pilate said to them, "Take Him your-
selves and crucify Him, for I find no crime in
Him."

The Jews answered him, "We have a law,
and by that law He ought to die, because He
has made Himself the Son of God."

When Pilate heard these words, he was
the more afraid; he entered the praetorium
again and said to Jesus, "Where are you
from?" But Jesus gave no answer. Pilate
therefore said to Him, "You will not speak to
me? Do You not know that I have power to
release You, and power to crucify You?"
Jesus answered him, "You would have no
power over Me unless it had been given you
from above."

John 19:6–11

*W*hen Pilate went to render judgment, he
was forced to entertain a possibility every
man and woman must face: Jesus claimed to be the
divine Son of God. Could it be true? What is to be
made of His claim?

Our Lord had pressed the issue some days before
with His disciples, asking, "Who do you say that I

am?" Peter had answered, "The Christ, the Son of the living God." Jesus responded that Peter could not have figured this out on his own; the heavenly Father had to reveal it (Matthew 16:16–7).

Pilate failed to find the grace to embrace such a revelation. Perhaps his mind was finally shut to it by his fear of an insurrection, with a loss of his own power and position. Perhaps wounded pride stood between him and the truth: This obstinate Man refused to admit that Pilate was in charge that day.

Whatever his reasons, Anne Catherine's vision reminds us that all who judge Christ will themselves be judged by Christ one day. Each of us, in responding to His claim to divinity, in answering His question, "Who do you say that I am?" is rendering a judgment on Him. As with Pilate, our eternal salvation hangs on the kind of judgment we ultimately make.

Pilate returned to the Praetorium, went alone into a room, and sent for our Savior. He glanced at the mangled and bleeding form before him and exclaimed inwardly: "Is it possible that He can be the Son of God?" Then he turned to Jesus and commanded Him to tell him whether He was God, whether He was the king who had been promised to the Jews, where His kingdom was, and to what class of gods He belonged.

Jesus' words were solemn and severe. He told Pilate that His kingdom was "not of this world," and He also spoke firmly of the many hidden crimes that defiled the conscience of the governor. He warned him of the dreadful fate that would be his if he did not repent. And He finally declared that He Himself, the Son of Man, would come at the last day, to pronounce a just judgment upon him.

Pilate was half frightened and half angry at the words of Jesus. He returned to the balcony and again declared that he would release Jesus. But the crowd cried out: "If you release this man, you are not Caesar's friend." Pilate saw that all his efforts were vain, and that he could make no impression on the infuriated mob. Their shouts and curses were deafening, and he began to fear an insurrection.

So he took water and washed his hands as the people watched, saying, "I am innocent of the blood of this righteous man; see to it yourselves."

The Dolorous Passion

Father, give me grace to confess Your Son daily
as my Lord and Judge.

III.

The Way of the Cross

24
Jesus Embraces the Cross

*You were dead in sins and uncircumcised in
the flesh. But God brought you back to life
with Christ, having forgiven us all our sins.
He has canceled our debt to the Law, which
had been charged against us. He obliterated
it by nailing it to the Cross. He disarmed the
demonic principalities and powers, parading
them publicly behind Him in the triumphal
procession of the Cross.*

Colossians 2:13–15*

*A*t the very heart of His sorrowful passion, we
have noted, Our Lord felt some sense of joy
because He knew the purpose of His suffering:
"Jesus ... for the joy that was set before Him,
endured the cross" (Hebrews 12:2). Yet we may still
find unsettling Maria's vision of Christ as He lifted
the cross to carry it. More than simply *enduring* it,
she saw Him *embracing* it, addressing it as "My
soul's beloved."

Could He have possibly been so enchanted by
the instrument of His death? The lives of certain
saints suggest that such could indeed have been the
case. Imitating Our Lord, they gave themselves up
to God in martyrdom, or in other forms of unsought

suffering, hoping like St. Paul to "complete what is lacking in Christ's afflictions" (Colossians 1:24). When they did, they too spoke passionately of whatever cross they were called to bear.

Recall, for example, the startling words of St. Ignatius of Antioch as he made his way in chains to the lions at Rome: "Come, fire, cross, battling with wild beasts, bones wrenched, limbs mangled, my whole body crushed, the Devil's cruel tortures—only let me get to Jesus Christ! ... Let me imitate the passion of my God. Whoever has Christ in them, let them appreciate what I am longing for."

As Maria's vision reveals, any delight Jesus may have taken in the Cross was in reality a delight in the brothers and sisters He would reconcile to God through it. His joy in suffering was a sign of His love for us.

Before He received the Cross, Jesus, the Master and Redeemer of the world, looked at it with the kind of joy and exultation that a bridegroom would display as he looks at his richly adorned bride. As the Cross was laid on Him, He addressed it this way:

"O Cross, My soul's beloved, now made ready to fulfill my desires—come to Me, so that I may be embraced in your arms, and so that, laid upon them as on an altar, I may be acceptable to the eternal Father as the sacrifice for His reconciliation with humanity. In order to embrace you, I have come down from heaven and taken on flesh that can suffer and die. You will be the scepter with which I will triumph over all My enemies, the key with which I will open the gates of heaven for all who have been chosen (Isaiah 22:22), the sanctuary where Adam's guilty sons will find mercy, and the treasure house that will lift them from poverty.

"In hanging on you, My Cross, I wish to lift up and urge on My friends the value of suffering the dishonor and reproach of the world. I want them to embrace such adversity joyfully, seek it eagerly, and follow Me on the path I will open up for them through you.

"Eternal Father, receive this sacrifice as acceptable to Your justice, so that from today on, they will not be servants anymore, but instead sons and heirs of Your kingdom with Me."

The Mystical City of God

Whatever cross You give me to carry, Father,
teach me to carry it with joy.

25
Jesus Meets His Mother

And His father and His mother marveled at what was said about Him; and Simeon blessed them and said to Mary His mother, "Behold, this Child is set for the fall and rising of many in Israel, and for a sign that is spoken against (and a sword will pierce through your own soul also), that thoughts out of many hearts may be revealed. ... And His mother kept all of these things in her heart.

Luke 2:34-35, 51

*J*esus had been only a few days old when the aged Simeon had warned His mother: Her Son would stir up trouble, and she would suffer deeply because of it. Surely she had pondered those words repeatedly over the years, as she had the events surrounding His birth (Luke 2:19). Once Jesus' public ministry had begun, she had no doubt recalled them with growing anxiety as she heard the insults, the threats, the denunciations that were hurled at Him with increasing malice.

Now, in the last tumultuous weeks of His life on earth, the anxiety had given way to anguish as Mary realized that the powers of darkness were gathering, and the hour had come. The sword had pricked her soul many times. Now, as her Son faced death, that sword was plunged to the depths.

In the traditional Stations of the Cross, Jesus meets Mary as He trudges through Jerusalem toward Calvary. In Maria's vision, mother and Son meet several times. The Gospel account suggests that she remained near Him in His suffering (John 19:25), so we can easily imagine that she would have found a place to stand along the street where she could try to catch His eye and cry out to Him.

Consider the scene: Any mother would be crushed to see her child endure so horrendous a passion. How much more, then, the mother of this Child, who loved so perfectly the One who was so worthy of perfect love!

At that moment of overwhelming grief, the ancient prophecy was finding its initial fulfillment: "When they look on Him whom they have pierced, they shall mourn for Him, as one mourns for an only child, and weep bitterly over Him, as one weeps over a firstborn" (Zechariah 12:10). In this way the Mother of Sorrows drew close to the Man of Sorrows (Isaiah 53:3), leaving an example for us all.

Through the swarms of the confused crowd, the angels led Mary to a sharp turn in the street, where she came face to face with her most holy Son. With deepest reverence she threw herself down before Him, adoring Him with a greater fervor, a deeper and more passionate reverence, than was ever given to Him before, or ever will be again, by any of His creatures. Then she stood up.

Mother and Son looked at each other with unspeakable tenderness, conversing with each other in their hearts as they were carried away by a sorrow too terrible to describe. Then this most wise lady stepped aside and followed Christ our Lord, continuing at a distance her inner communion with her Son and with the eternal Father.

The image of her divine Son, so horribly wounded, defiled, and bound, remained firmly fixed and imprinted on her soul. Throughout her lifetime it never faded. It remained in her mind as vividly as if she were beholding Him ceaselessly with her own eyes.

With a most bitter grief, she spoke to the Lord in her heart: "My Son and eternal God, light of my eyes and life of my soul: Accept, my Lord, this sacrifice, that I am not able to take the burden of the Cross from You and carry it myself. O infinite, sweetest love, I wish that the hearts and wills of all people were mine. Then they would be unable to show such ingratitude for all that You are suffering!"

The Mystical City of God

Jesus, teach me how to draw close to You as Your mother did by joining my sufferings to Yours.

26
St. Simon Carries the Cross

When they had mocked Him, they stripped Him of the robe, and put His own clothes on Him, and led Him away to crucify Him. As they were marching out, they came upon a man of Cyrene, Simon by name; this man they compelled to carry his cross.

Matthew 27:31–32

*C*onsider now Simon of Cyrene, the Everyman of the passion story. Like so many of us, he is a mere passerby as the great events of this world take place, an anonymous shadow ignored by the famous and powerful. He is unknown, uninterested in being known, and carefully minding his own business. But one day he happens to pass too close; the great events swallow him up; and before it is all over, the Everyman becomes the Holy Man, both hero and saint.

In the Simon of Anne Catherine's vision we gaze into an all-too-truthful mirror. Like most of us, he was not prepared to be inconvenienced. He had things to do, places to go, children to care for, and a spouse waiting impatiently at home.

He resented helping a total stranger, especially when he had no choice. Charity isn't charity, he may have mumbled to himself, when it's coerced. Worse yet, the Man he had to assist looked repulsive, abhor-rent—a bloody, filthy criminal.

Yet with one look into Jesus' eyes, everything changed for Simon. His heart began to melt, and before long, he was carrying that Cross to a new eternal destiny. So it is with us: God honors even the most reluctant acts of charity with abundant grace, and so we inch toward sainthood in the situations we were least expecting.

The procession had reached an arch formed in an old wall belonging to the town, opposite to a square, in which three streets terminated, when Jesus stumbled against a large stone placed in the middle of the archway. The Cross slipped from His shoulder, He fell upon the stone, and He was totally unable to rise.

This fall caused a fresh delay, as our Lord could not stand up again. So the Pharisees said to the soldiers: "We'll never get Him to the place of execution alive if you don't find someone to carry His cross."

At this moment Simon of Cyrene, a pagan, happened to pass by, accompanied by his three chil-dren. He was a gardener, just returning home after working in a garden near the eastern wall of the city.

He was carrying a bundle of lopped branches.

The soldiers, perceiving by his dress that he was a pagan, seized him, and ordered him to assist Jesus in carrying His cross. He refused at first, but he was soon compelled to obey. His children, being frightened, cried and made a great noise, so some women quieted them and took charge of them.

Simon was quite annoyed, and he expressed the greatest irritation at being made to walk with a man in so deplorable a condition of dirt and misery. But Jesus wept and cast such a mild and heavenly look upon him that he was touched. Instead of continuing to show reluctance, he instead helped Him to rise, while the executioners fastened one arm of the cross on his shoulders.

In this way Simon walked behind our Lord, relieving Him to a great extent from its weight; and when everything was arranged, the procession moved forward. Simon had not carried the cross after Jesus for very long before he felt his heart deeply touched by grace.

The Dolorous Passion

Show me, Lord, those all around me who need help carrying their burdens.

27
Jesus Is Stripped Naked

And they stripped [Jesus] and put a scarlet robe upon Him, and plaiting a crown of thorns they put it on His head, and put a reed in His right hand. ... And when they had mocked Him, they stripped Him of the robe, and put His own clothes on Him, and led Him away to crucify Him. ... And when they had crucified Him, they divided His garments among them.

Matthew 27:28–29, 31, 35

*J*esus' tormentors intended to wound more than His body; they sought to wound His soul as well. So the beatings and scourging, nails and thorns were wrapped in insults and curses, mockery and laughter. The goal was humiliation; and the goal was most clearly displayed when, again and again, they stripped Him naked in public.

Yet there is a bittersweet irony here. Ever since the sin of our first parents in Eden, nakedness had been linked to shame: "I heard You in the garden," Adam had said to God, "and I was afraid, because I was naked; so I hid myself" (Genesis 3:10*). But here, for the first time since the Fall, stood a Man without sin. Our Lord, the new Adam (1 Corinthians

15:45–49) was also naked, but He was not ashamed. He had nothing to hide.

Instead, Jesus' nakedness revealed the blessed Body that was broken and given for our salvation. In stripping Him, His enemies were in fact unwrapping for us the Bread of heaven (John 6:51).

Maria's vision details the wounds that flowed as Jesus' tunic was torn away, and to the eyes of faith those wounds shine with a bloody beauty. For in this despicable act of humiliation, unwitting men unveiled the awesome humility of God. The divine nakedness was exposed so that the shame of our race might be taken away.

Laid bare on Mount Calvary is Christ's full humanity, covering for a season His full Divinity. There we see compelling evidence that He has taken our nature and joined it to His nature; that our flesh and blood have truly become His Flesh and Blood. And on that day when we stand, God willing, before the throne of heaven, we will behold there—naked, unobscured, clothed only in unutterable glory—the familiar, precious wounds of One of our own.

It was noon, and the executioners, who intended to crucify Him naked, stripped Him of His seamless tunic and His other clothes. The tunic was large and without an opening in the front, so they pulled it over Jesus' head without taking off the crown of thorns. Because of the brutality they showed as they performed this task, they cruelly ripped off the crown with the tunic.

In this way they opened up again all His head wounds, and in some of these the thorns at first remained embedded. But even though the thorns were sharp and hard, they were eventually wrenched from His head by the violence with which the executioners tore off His tunic, and with it, the crown. Then, with inhuman brutality they forced it down once more on His sacred head, opening wounds upon wounds.

The brutal ripping of the tunic also opened up again the wounds of His entire body, because the bloody cloth had dried into the open places so that its removal added new pains to His wounds. Four times during the Passion they stripped Jesus of His clothing, and then dressed Him again. The first time was to scourge Him at the pillar; the second, to wrap Him in the mock scarlet; the third, when they took off the scarlet to dress Him again in His tunic; and the fourth, when they finally took away His clothes before they crucified Him.

This last stripping was the most painful. His wounds were more numerous, His holy humanity was more weakened, and there was less protection against the biting wind on Mount Calvary.

The Mystical City of God

Father, I stand naked before You, and there is no place to hide; clothe me in the holiness of Your Son.

28
Jesus Prays for Us All

*Jesus lifted up His eyes to heaven and said,
"Father, the hour has come; glorify Your Son
so that the Son may glorify You, since You
have given Him power over all flesh, to give
eternal life to all whom You have given Him.
... I do not pray that You would take them out
of the world, but that You would keep them
from the evil one. ... For their sake I consecrate Myself, that they also may be conse-
crated in truth. ... I do not pray for these
only, but also for those who believe in Me
through their word."*

John 17:1–2, 15, 19–20*

*W*hat thoughts filled Our Lord's mind as He waited to receive the nails in His hands? Was He thinking of His innocence ... His pain ... the fast-approaching moment of His death?

Given the words He had prayed a few hours before (recorded in John chapter 17), we should not be surprised that in Maria's vision, Jesus was thinking of none of those things at that moment. Instead, His thoughts turned, as they had in Gethsemane, to His Father in heaven and to those for whom He was laying down His life. Our Lord was interceding: for His mother, His followers, His enemies, the world.

As the executioners prepared the Cross, then, He was praying for you, for me, and for us all.

What gifts did He ask for us? What graces did He beg for us? He asked that we be granted mercy instead of condemnation. He prayed for our deliverance from Satan's slavery. He begged to save us and make a place for us in the family of God. And He revealed once more His passion to accomplish the salvation of man for the glory of God.

Yet there was one more grace Jesus requested, Maria tells us. So that we might be prepared to receive such extraordinary gifts, He prayed that you and I would meditate on His passion with a loving heart. In our present reflections, then, Christ's own prayer, at least in part, is being answered.

The holy Cross was lying on the ground, and the executioners were at work with the preparations needed to crucify Jesus and the two thieves. As they did, our Redeemer and Master prayed to the Father this way:

"Eternal Father, My Lord God, I offer My complete humanity to the majesty of Your infinite goodness and justice, which is beyond all understanding.

I offer all that I have accomplished according to Your will in coming down from Your bosom to take on suffering, mortal flesh for the redemption of men, My brethren.

"I consecrate to You, Lord, along with Myself, My most loving mother. I offer You the little flock of My apostles, the holy Church and the assembly of the faithful—as it is now, and as it will be to the end of the world. With it, I offer You all the mortal children of Adam.

"It is my wish that I may suffer and die for all, and I desire that all will be saved if they will follow Me and benefit from My redemption. In this way they will be freed from slavery to the Devil and become Your children, My brethren, and co-heirs of the grace I have merited.

"I beg You, My Father, to withhold Your chastisement and to hold back from men the scourge of Your justice. Do not let them be punished for their sins as they deserve.

"I pray for those who are persecuting Me. Grant that they may be converted to the truth.

"From now on, be their Father as You are Mine. I beg You also to grant them grace to meditate on My death in devout affection, and to be enlightened from heaven.

"Above all, I ask You to glorify Your most holy name."

The Mystical City of God

In every way, Jesus, let my life become an answer to Your prayers for the world.

29
Jesus Is Crucified

When they came to a place called Golgotha (which means the place of a skull), they offered Him wine to drink, mingled with gall; but when He tasted it, He would not drink it. And when they had crucified Him, they divided His garments among them by casting lots; then they sat down and kept watch over Him there. And over His head they put the charge against Him, which read, "This is Jesus the King of the Jews." Then two robbers were crucified with Him, one on the right and one on the left.

Matthew 27:33–38

Speaking of His death, Jesus had once solemnly told His disciples: "I, when I am lifted up from the earth, will draw all men to Myself" (John 12:32–33). His prophecy was now fulfilled. As the Cross was raised atop Calvary's hill, multitudes were quickly drawn to Him.

Some—a mob of His enemies—were there to jeer and celebrate. Others, such as His mother, were there to wail and mourn. Still others watched in curiosity, morbidly fascinated by the brutal scene, not yet able to love Him or hate Him, though unable as well to turn away.

Today our attention is still riveted on the Man of the Cross. He draws us all to Himself. We may cherish Him, we may despise Him, we may puzzle over Him. But we cannot ignore Him. Even when He is naked, filthy, bloody, dying—precisely because He is these things—we cannot remain indifferent once we have seen Him lifted up from the earth.

Sooner or later, gathered around the Cross, we each must choose: Will we take our stand with the mother or with the mob? Even the curious, if they watch long enough, eventually find that the curiosity either corrodes into animosity or ripens into affection. For the latter, Anne Catherine insisted, the Cross becomes a tree of life.

The executioners offered Jesus some vinegar and gall. But He turned away from it in silence. Then they told Him to place himself on the Cross so they could nail Him to it. During the whole time of the crucifixion, Our Lord never ceased praying and repeating those prophetic passages in the Psalms that He was then fulfilling, although from time to time a feeble moan caused by His extreme suffering could be heard. In this manner He had prayed when carrying His cross, and thus He continued to pray until His death.

When the executioners had finished the crucifixion of our Lord, they erected the Cross. It was at once a terrible but touching sight to behold the Cross raised up in the midst of the vast multitude of people who were assembled all around. Not only insulting soldiers, proud Pharisees, and the brutal mob were there, but also strangers from all parts.

The air resounded with shouts of derision when they saw the Cross towering on high. But words of love and compassion echoed through the air at the same moment. These words, of course, came from the most saintly of human beings: Mary, John, the holy women, and all who were pure of heart.

Thus was the blessed Cross of Our Lord planted for the first time on the earth. Well might it be compared to the tree of life in Paradise, for the wounds of Jesus were like sacred fountains, from which flowed four rivers destined both to purify the world from the curse of sin, and to give it fertility, in order to produce fruit to salvation.

The Dolorous Passion

Jesus, draw me to Your cross to drink from the fountain of life.

30
"Father, Forgive Them"

*Jesus said, "Father, forgive them; for they
know not what they do." And they cast lots to
divide His garments. And the people stood
by, watching; but the rulers scoffed at Him,
saying, "He saved others; let Him save
Himself, if He is the Christ of God, His
Chosen One!" The soldiers also mocked
Him, coming up and offering Him vinegar,
and saying, "If you are the King of the Jews,
save Yourself!"*

Luke 23:34–37

*S*t. Peter once asked Our Lord how many times
he must forgive an offender. Jesus answered
that if necessary, he must forgive "seventy times
seven" (Matthew 18:22). Certainly by the time Jesus
mounted the Cross, the number of savage blows He
had sustained well exceeded even that figure. Thus
was He able to illustrate His instruction by stunning
example when He spoke His first words from the
Cross: "Father, forgive them."

Since early times, teachers of the Church have
viewed the Cross, not only as the throne of the great
King, but also as the lectern of the great Teacher. On
the Cross, the words of His metaphors and parables,

like the divine Word Himself, took on flesh and entered history. The builders rejected the Stone (Matthew 21:42); the Shepherd gave His life for the sheep (John 10:11–15); the vineyard owner's Son was murdered by the tenants (Matthew 21:33–41); the kernel died in order to bear a harvest (John 12:24).

According to Maria, Jesus not only embodied His teaching perfectly; He refused to give His disciples any test that He Himself had not passed. When He called out to God to pardon His tormentors and murderers, He was passing such a test, answering with a resounding *Yes!* the question that had lingered in the back of His disciples' minds: Is such costly forgiveness truly possible?

The Pharisees and the priests, forgetting about the two robbers, focused all the poison of their rage on the sinless, holy One. Wagging their heads scornfully in mockery, they threw rocks and dirt at the royal Lord and His Cross, saying: "You who can destroy the temple and rebuild it in three days, save Yourself now! He saved others; let Him save Himself! If this is the Son of God, let Him come down from the Cross, and we will believe in Him!" (Matthew 27:39–42).

The wood of the Cross formed the throne of

Christ's majesty and the lectern for the Teacher of life. He had now mounted that throne, that lectern, to confirm His teaching by His example. Christ now uttered those words of the highest, most perfect love: "Father, forgive them, for they know not what they do!"

The divine Teacher had made His own this principle of charity and brotherly love, and He had taught it by His own lips (Matthew 18:21–22; John 15:12–13). Now He confirmed and carried it out on the Cross. Not only did He forgive and love His enemies. He even went so far as to excuse, under the plea of ignorance, those whose malice had reached the most extreme forms humanly possible in persecuting, blaspheming, and crucifying their God and Redeemer.

Such was the difference between the actions of ungrateful men who had been favored with such great enlightenment, teaching, and blessing, and the actions of Jesus in His most fiery charity while enduring the crown of thorns, the nails, the Cross, and unparalleled blasphemy at human hands. O love beyond understanding! O sweetness beyond description! O patience beyond human imagining, yet worthy of the angels' admiration and the devils' terror!

The Mystical City of God

Father, forgive us our trespasses, as we forgive those who trespass against us.

31
One Thief Repents

When they came to the place which is called The Skull, there they crucified Him, and the criminals, one on the right and one on the left. ... One of the criminals who were hanged railed at Him, saying, "Are You not the Christ? Save Yourself and us!"

But the other rebuked him, saying, "Do you not fear God, since you are under the same sentence of condemnation? And we indeed justly; for we are receiving the due reward of our deeds; but this Man has done nothing wrong." And he said, "Jesus, remember me when You come into Your kingdom."

And He said to him, "Truly, I say to you, today you will be with Me in Paradise."

Luke 23:33; 39–43

*T*he two thieves crucified with Christ hang before us like a microcosm of Judgment Day. Enthroned on His Cross between them is the Judge, with the "sheep" at His right hand and the "goat" at His left—one on his way to eternal life, and the other to everlasting punishment (Matthew 25:31–46).

We know little about these two men, though tradition has given the name Dismas to the "good thief" and the name "Gestas" to the other. Legend has embroidered their story with tales of an encounter between them and the Holy Family, many years before, in Egypt. Anne Catherine's vision displays one version of that story. But she focuses, as the Gospels do, on their final moments, when their eternal fate hangs in the balance.

Dismas' example gives to even the worst of us a reason for hope, and a motive for humility. As St. Augustine summed it up: "Do not despair; one of the thieves was saved; do not presume; one of the thieves was damned."

The thieves suffered terribly, and the one on the left never ceased cursing and swearing. The face and indeed the whole body of Jesus was drained of color; He appeared to be about to faint. The wicked thief exclaimed, "The demon who has possessed Him is about to leave Him!" Then he cried out to Jesus, "If You are the Christ, save Yourself and us!"

Dismas, the good thief, was silent, but he was deeply moved at the prayer of Jesus to forgive His enemies. Our Lord's prayers obtained for him a most powerful grace; he exclaimed to the other thief in a loud and clear voice, "How can you insult Him when He prays for you? He has been silent, and suffered all your outrages with patience. He is truly a prophet—He is our king—He is the Son of God!"

This unexpected reproof from the lips of a miserable criminal dying on a cross caused a tremendous commotion among the spectators. They gathered up stones and intended to throw them at him. But the centurion would not allow it.

Dismas said to the other thief, who was still blaspheming Jesus: "Don't you fear God, since You are under the same condemnation? We indeed are justly condemned, for we receive the due reward of our deeds. But this Man has done no evil. Remember that you are now at the point of death, and repent."

The good thief was enlightened and touched. He confessed his sins to Jesus and said, "Lord, if You condemn me, it will be with justice."

Jesus replied, "You will experience My mercy." Then Dismas, filled with the most perfect contrition, began right away to thank God for the great graces he had received, and to reflect on the many sins of his past life.

The Dolorous Passion

Lord Jesus Christ, Son of God,
have mercy on me, a sinner.

32
Darkness Over the Land

It was now about the sixth hour, and there was darkness over the whole land until the ninth hour, while the sun's light failed.

Luke 23:44–45

*W*hen God made the heavenly bodies, He declared: "Let them be for signs and ... to give light upon the earth" (Genesis 1:14–15). On the day Jesus was crucified, when the midday sun hid its face in shame and refused to perform its assigned task, it was indeed a sign: The "Sun of Righteousness" Himself (Malachi 4:2) had been eclipsed by the sin of the world.

Anne Catherine elaborated on that sign. She saw the whole cosmos, from the little sparrows to the immense galaxies, injured and crippled by this assault on its Creator and Sustainer. If it is true that, as St. Paul said, "in Him all things hold together" (Colossians 1:16), then surely at His death, all things were falling apart.

But there was more. The darkness, the visionary insisted, was also a mirror of the blackness that descended over the interior landscape of Our Lord. To gaze on the deep murkiness that wrapped the land and the people was thus to catch a glimpse of the terrible abyss into which His soul was plummeting.

Even so, the darkest hour is just before dawn, and this gloom was a sign as well that the "Dawn from on high" was close at hand—"to give light to those who sit in darkness and in the shadow of death" (Luke 1:78). In that hour Our Lord prayed for God's will to be done, so that even in the catastrophic darkness, the heavens might "proclaim His handiwork" (Psalm 19:1).

The sun was suddenly darkened. I was lifted up from the earth, and beheld the stars and the planets moving around out of their proper spheres. I saw the moon like an immense ball of fire rolling along as if flying from the earth. I was then suddenly taken back to Jerusalem, and I beheld the moon reappear behind the Mount of Olives, looking pale and full, and advancing rapidly towards the sun, which was dim and shrouded by a fog. The sky grew darker, and the stars appeared to cast a red and lurid light.

I was taken into Jerusalem to see what was going on there. The inhabitants were totally overcome with terror and anxiety. The streets were dark and gloomy, and some people were feeling their way around, while others, seated on the ground with their heads veiled, struck their breasts, or went up to the roofs of their houses, looked at the sky, and burst out in bitter mourning. Even the animals issued mournful cries and hid themselves; the birds flew low and fell to the ground.

The consternation produced by the sudden darkness at Mount Calvary was indescribable. Every sound ceased, each voice was hushed, and remorse and terror took possession of every heart. Stillness reigned around the Cross; Jesus hung upon it all alone.

His soul was overwhelmed with an indescribable feeling of bitterness and grief. Everything inside Him was dark, gloomy, and wretched. Thus the darkness that reigned all around Him was only a symbol of the interior darkness He endured.

Even so, Our Lord turned to His heavenly Father. He prayed for His enemies; He offered the chalice of His sufferings for their redemption; He continued to pray as He had done during the whole of His passion; and He repeated the Psalms whose prophecies were at that moment receiving their fulfillment in Him.

The Dolorous Passion

Sun of Righteousness, when darkness overwhelms my soul, shine on me with healing in Your wings.

33
"Behold Your Mother"

When Jesus saw His mother, and the disciple whom He loved standing near, He said to His mother, "Woman, behold, your son!" Then He said to the disciple, "Behold, your mother!" And from that hour the disciple took her to his own home.

John 19:25–27

*W*e may find it startling to hear Jesus address Mary, not as "Mother," but as "Woman," in His last words to her before He died. Some have suggested that in their culture, such a form of address would not have been unusual or rude. But there seems to be something more at work here, something that demands further explanation.

Commenting on this situation, Maria insisted that in calling the Virgin "Woman," Our Lord was alluding to her perfect womanhood, her status as the exemplar for all women. He wished to say to her: "You are the Woman blessed among all women, the most wise among all the daughters of Adam; you are Woman, strong and faithful, unconquered by sin."

Anne Catherine perceives yet another layer of meaning in the word, seeing in it a reference to the woman who would crush the serpent's head through her seed (Genesis 3:15)—a prophecy that, even then, was coming to pass. In entrusting her to John, perhaps Our Lord was also pointing to John's future vision, when he would behold "a woman clothed with the sun," whose crucified Son would one day rule the nations (Revelation 12:1–2).

In any case, Anne Catherine notes, the Woman became on that day the mother of the Church. The first Christians "had all things in common" (Acts 2:44), including the mother who had prayed with them and for them on the Day of Pentecost (Acts 1:14). If her Son was "not ashamed to call them brethren" (Hebrews 1:11), then calling them all her children would be her delight.

Jesus turned His head toward John and said, "Woman, behold your son." Then He said to John, "Behold your mother." John looked at his dying Redeemer and bowed his head in the most respectful way to honor this beloved mother, whom he ever after considered as his own.

It did not appear to me in the least surprising that Jesus should call the Blessed Virgin "Woman" instead of "Mother." I felt that He intended to demonstrate that she was that woman spoken of in Scripture who was to crush the head of the serpent

(Genesis 3:15), and that this was the very moment in which that promise was accomplished in the death of her Son. I also knew that Jesus, by giving her as a mother to John, gave her also as a mother to all who believe in Him, who become children of God and are not born of flesh and blood, nor of the will of man, but of God (John 1:12–13).

Mary was the most pure, the most humble, and the most obedient among women, the one who, when hailed by the angel as "full of grace," had immediately replied, "Behold the handmaid of the Lord; let it be to me according to your word" (Luke 1:38). At that time, in her sacred womb the Word had been instantly made flesh. So it did not seem surprising to me, either, that when she was informed by her dying Son that she was to become the spiritual mother of another son, she would repeat those words with humble obedience and immediately adopt as her children all the children of God, the brothers of Jesus Christ.

The Dolorous Passion

Jesus, my Brother, I thank You for giving me Your mother to be my own.

34
"Why Have You Forsaken Me?"

About three o'clock Jesus cried with a loud voice, "Eli, Eli, lama sabach-thani?" which means, "My God, My God, why have You forsaken Me?"

Matthew 27:46*

*J*esus' cry from the cross that God had forsaken Him should perplex us: How is it possible that God the Father could have abandoned God the Son? Could such a rift actually tear through the heart of the Blessed Trinity?

We may never enter fully into the tremendous mystery presented here, but we should note that He was crying out the words of a Psalm whose several details had prophesied His death (Psalm 22). Some have speculated that, since Christ bore our sins in that moment, a perfectly holy God turned His face away as part of the punishment Jesus suffered in our place. Others have insisted that the Father was always present; but in His agony, Jesus in His human nature had lost His awareness of that Presence.

Anne Catherine envisions yet another possibility: Christ, she said, was speaking on behalf of all those who in their hour of death are tempted to despair. He has walked the way before them, borne their desperate hopelessness, and earned for them a sure and certain hope.

Jesus' sufferings were inexpressible. But it was through them that He merited for us the grace necessary to resist the temptations to despair that will assail us at the hour of death—that dreadful hour when we will feel that we are about to leave all that is dear to us here below.

When our minds, weakened by disease, have lost the power of reasoning, and even our hopes of mercy and forgiveness have become, it seems, enveloped in mist and uncertainty, then it is that we must fly to Jesus. We must unite our feelings of desolation with that unspeakable abandonment He endured on the cross, and be certain of obtaining a glorious victory over our enemies from hell. In that moment, Jesus offered to His eternal Father His forsakenness.

For this reason, no one who is united to Jesus in the bosom of His Church must despair at the awful moment preceding his departure from this life, even if he is deprived of all light and comfort of the senses. For he must then remember that the Christian is no longer obliged to enter this dark desert alone and unprotected. Since Jesus has cast His own interior and exterior abandonment on the

Cross into this gulf of desolation, the Christian will not be left to cope alone with death, or be allowed to leave this world in desolation of spirit, deprived of heavenly consolation.

All fear of loneliness and despair in death must therefore be cast away. For Jesus, who is our true Light, the Way, the Truth, and the Life, has gone before us on that dreary road, has scattered it with blessings, and has raised His Cross on it. Just one glance at that Cross will calm our every fear.

In His cry of abandonment, then, Jesus (if we may put it this way) made His last will and testament in the presence of His Father, bequeathing the merits of His death and passion to the Church and to sinners. The cry He allowed to pass His lips in the height of His agony was intended not only to show the enormity of His sufferings, but also to encourage all afflicted souls who acknowledge God as their Father to lay their sorrows at His feet with the confidence of a child.

The Dolorous Passion

Now, as in my hour of death, Lord Jesus,
I place all my trust in You.

IV

"I Make All Things New"

35
All Is Now Finished

> *After this Jesus, knowing that all was now finished, said (to fulfill the Scripture), "I thirst." A bowl full of vinegar stood there; so they put a sponge full of the vinegar on hyssop and held it to His mouth. When Jesus had received the vinegar, He said, "It is finished!"*
>
> John 19:28–30

*B*efore Jesus gave up His spirit to the Father, He cried out two brief declarations: "I thirst" and "It is finished." Though we may not easily see the relation between them, St. John hints at their inner unity. Only when Our Lord knew "that all was now finished," the evangelist writes, was He able to declare "I thirst," receive the vinegar, and pronounce the consummation of His life's work.

Maria explored this mysterious connection by unfolding the depths of these two statements. Christ's most profound thirst, she said, was His passionate longing for the salvation of the human race. In this moment, the pinnacle of His earthly mission, His thirst for souls had become unbearable. Though only hours before He had prayed that this cup might pass, now He cried aloud one last time so that He might be able to drink it to the dregs.

He did indeed drink it, and at last He was satisfied. In "I thirst," we hear the groan of divine desire; in "It is finished," a cry of desire fulfilled.

"I thirst!" Jesus was expressing a most exalted mystery: He was thirsting to see Adam's captive children make use of the liberty He had merited for them and offered them—a liberty so many were abusing. He was thirsty with an eager desire for all to communicate with Him with the faith and love He deserved, so that they would gain by His merits and passion. He wanted them to accept the friendship and grace now being purchased for them, so that they would not lose the everlasting happiness that He was to bequeath to those who wanted to accept it and be made fit for it.

But His treacherous enemies and His executioners, displaying their unhappy and hardened hearts, attached a sponge soaked in vinegar to a reed and lifted it, mockingly, to His mouth, so that He could drink it. In this way was fulfilled the prophecy of David: "For my thirst they gave me vinegar to drink" (Psalm 69:21).

In connection with this same mystery, the Savior then declared: "It is finished! Now this work of My advent from heaven is completed. I have obeyed the command of My eternal Father, who sent Me to suffer and die for the salvation of the world. Now the holy Scriptures are fulfilled—the prophecies and the figures of the Old Testament. Now the course of My earthly, mortal life, which I assumed in the womb of My mother, is finished.

"Now My example, My teachings, My sacraments, and My remedies for the sickness of sin are established on earth. Now the justice of My eternal Father in regard to the debt of Adam's children is satisfied. Now My holy Church is endowed with the cures for the sins committed by men.

"The whole work of My coming as the Restorer of the world is completed insofar as it concerns My earthly life. Now the sure foundation of the Church Triumphant has been laid in the Church Militant, and nothing can overthrow it or alter it." These are the mysteries contained in the words: "It is finished!"

The Mystical City of God

Lord, let my soul be a drop in the cup that quenches Your thirst.

36
The Moment of Triumph

*Then Jesus, crying with a loud voice, said,
"Father, into Your hands I commit My
spirit!" And having said this, He breathed
His last. Now when the centurion saw what
had taken place, he praised God, and said,
"Certainly this man was innocent!" And all
the multitudes who assembled to see the
sight, when they saw what had taken place,
returned home beating their breasts.*

Luke 23:46–48

*J*esus' last words on the cross are a shout of
triumphant faith. The earlier cry of abandonment has now given way to a declaration of supreme
confidence in God. Without hesitation, the Son
entrusts Himself totally to His Father.

Nor was it a passive surrender. As St. John
Chrysostom noted, the Gospel of John contains an
important detail in this regard. Usually a man
dies, Chrysostom observed, and then his lifeless
head bends down. But according to the Gospel,
Jesus bowed His head first, and then died (John
19:30)—a sign that He was laying down His life
willingly. "No one takes My life from Me," He
had told His disciples, "but I lay it down of My

own accord" (John 10:18).

In Matthew's account especially, we find evidence that these last words were less the last gasp of a Victim than the trumpet of a victorious Warrior King preparing to return home from battle: "And behold, the curtain of the temple was torn in two, from top to bottom; and the earth shook, and the rocks were split; the tombs also were opened, and many bodies of the saints who had fallen asleep were raised" (Matthew 27:51–52).

Anne Catherine's vision focuses on this militant aspect of Our Lord's death. The brave centurion submits to his new Commander, and countless other hearts as well are conquered by His grace. The earth trembles beneath her Lord's advance, the saints of old are released from prison, and the ancient Enemy is at last utterly overthrown.

Lifting His head, Jesus cried out in a loud voice, "Father, into Your hands I commit My spirit!" These words, which He uttered in a clear and thrilling tone, resounded through heaven and earth. A moment afterward, He bowed down His head and gave up His spirit.

When Our Lord pronounced His last words in a thunderous shout before dying, the earth trembled, and the rock of Calvary burst apart, forming a deep chasm between the cross of our Lord and the cross of the impenitent thief. The voice of God—that solemn and terrible voice—had reverberated through the whole universe, breaking the solemn silence that had pervaded all nature. Jesus' last cry filled every breast with terror. The convulsed earth paid homage to its Creator; the sword of grief pierced the hearts of those who loved Him.

This moment was the moment of grace for the centurion. From this moment on he was a new man; he adored the true God and would no longer serve His enemies. Many others among the spectators were also truly converted.

I saw the soul of Jesus, at the moment He died, appear like a bright orb. Accompanied by angels, including Gabriel, it penetrated the earth at the foot of the Cross. I also saw these angels cast a number of evil spirits into the great abyss. And I heard Jesus order several of the souls in the underworld to reenter the bodies in which they once dwelled so that the sight might fill sinners with a healthy terror, and these souls might give a solemn testimony to His divinity.

The Dolorous Passion

Crucified Lord, the earth welcomes You
as conquering King.

37
Satan Is Defeated

*Since therefore the children share in flesh
and blood, [Christ] Himself likewise partook
of the same nature, that through death He
might destroy him who has the power of
death, that is, the Devil, and deliver all those
who through fear of death were subject to
lifelong bondage.*

Hebrews 2:14–15

*A*ncient Christian teachers sometimes spoke
wryly of the Incarnation as God's fishing
expedition to snare the Devil. For ages, Satan had
gone about devouring human souls as a ferocious
shark devours little fish. But now the Devil himself
would become the prey.

As this intriguing image pictures it, God cast
Christ into the sea of the world. Satan thought Christ
was just another soul, and he intended to consume
Him through death as he had consumed so many
others. But Our Lord's human nature was in fact
simply the bait. Hidden within it, unknown to the
Devil, was the hook of Christ's divine nature. Not
even a shark was big enough or strong enough to
swallow that.

Satan took the bait; he stirred up Christ's enemies

to crucify Him. But the Devil got much more than he bargained for. When he tried to swallow the sinless Man at death, he hooked himself on the holy God concealed there. The Evil One knew now that he had made a fatal mistake, but it was too late. God reeled him in for good.

Maria insisted, as did those ancient Christians, that Lucifer was blinded by his own pride to the reality of Christ's true identity until the end of His life. God was working through the humble Carpenter of Nazareth to accomplish the total overthrow of the kingdom of darkness. But as St. Paul wrote, "None of the [demonic] rulers of this age understood this; for if they had, they would not have crucified the Lord of glory" (1 Corinthians 2:8).

Maria's vision takes us to that moment, as Jesus was dying, when the hosts of hell finally figured out what was going on. Despite their maniacal rage at having been outwitted and defeated, they were powerless to resist divine judgment. God's justice snatched them out of this world and cast them into an eternal torment of their own making. At long last, the human race could be free.

Through Christ's words on the Cross, Lucifer and his hordes learned at last that the mystery of the Incarnation and the Redemption had now been accomplished and made perfectly complete according to God's wise decree. They were made to sense that Christ our Redeemer, in all obedience, had fulfilled the will of the eternal Father. He had brought to pass all the promises and prophecies made to the world by the fathers of old.

His humility and obedience had made up for their own arrogance and rebellion in heaven when they had refused to submit themselves and acknowledge Him as their Superior in human flesh. Now, through the wisdom of God, they were brought low and defeated by the same Lord they had despised.

The immense dignity and the infinite merits of Christ demanded that in this very moment He should carry out His authority and power as Judge over angels and men—an office granted to Him by the eternal Father. Now He applied this power by hurling this sentence at Lucifer and all his followers: Condemned to eternal fire, they must immediately depart into the deepest dungeons of hell. The casting down of Lucifer and his demons from Calvary to the abyss was even more violent and calamitous than their initial expulsion from heaven.

The Mystical City of God

O my Jesus, forgive us of our sins, save us from the fires of hell; lead all souls to heaven, especially those in most need of Thy mercy.

38
Blood and Water

One of the soldiers pierced His side with a spear, and at once there came out blood and water. ... For these things took place that the Scripture might be fulfilled ... "They shall look on Him whom they have pierced."

John 19:34–37

*O*ur Lord's suffering had at last come to an end. But the graces flowing from His passion had only just begun to flood the world. They sprang first from the precious fountain of His heart, pierced by the soldier's lance.

Just as Eve was created from the side of "the first Adam," so the Church draws her life from the side of "the last Adam" (1 Corinthians 15:45). Since ancient times, the Church fathers have seen in this "blood and water" the font of two life-giving sacraments, Baptism and the Eucharist. Through these mysteries the Church is established, and through these the life of her crucified Lord is communicated to all generations.

In Catherine Anne's vision, a minor Roman officer comes to symbolize the power of the sacraments in the Church to come. Grace prompts him to approach the Body of Christ; grace heals and enlightens him through the Blood and Water he finds

165

there; and grace compels him to gather the Gifts he has received to share them with the world.

The armed men still appeared doubtful whether Jesus was really dead. The brutality they had shown in breaking the legs of the thieves who had still been alive made the holy women tremble to consider what outrage they might next perpetrate on the body of our Lord.

Cassius, a young, lower-ranking Roman officer was nearby. His weak, squinting eyes and nervous manner had often provoked the derision of his companions. But he was suddenly illuminated by grace, and being quite overcome at the sight of the cruel conduct of the soldiers, and the deep sorrow of the holy women, he determined to relieve their anxiety by proving beyond dispute that Jesus was really dead.

The kindness of his heart prompted him, but unknowingly he fulfilled a prophecy. He seized his lance and rode quickly up to the mound on which the Cross was planted. Then, taking his lance in both hands, he thrust it so deeply into the right side of Jesus that the point went through the heart and appeared on the left side.

When Cassius drew his lance out of the wound, a

quantity of blood and water rushed from it and flowed over his face and body. This washing produced effects much like those of the life-giving waters of baptism: Grace and salvation at once entered his soul. He leapt from his horse, threw himself upon his knees, struck his breast, and confessed loudly before everyone his firm belief in the divinity of Jesus. Cassius also thanked God because the problem with his eyes had been healed at the same moment the darkness had been dispersed from his soul.

Every heart was overcome at the sight of the blood of our Lord, which ran into a hollow in the rock at the foot of the cross. Mary, John, the holy women, and Cassius gathered up the blood and water in flasks and wiped up the remainder with pieces of linen. The water and blood continued to flow from the large wound in the side of our Lord; it ran into the hollow in the rock, and the holy women put it in vases, while Mary and Mary Magdalene mingled their tears.

The Dolorous Passion

Deep in Your precious Body, Jesus, hide me;
let me never forsake the graces that flow
there from Your heart.

39
"Follow Me!"

Then Jesus told His disciples, "If any man would come after Me, let him deny himself and take up his cross and follow Me. For whoever would save his life will lose it, and whoever loses his life for My sake will find it."

Matthew 16:24–25

*T*he old saying bears repeating: God's grace is free, but it costs us everything.

Many of us seem to want just enough grace to "get by." Not enough to make us uncomfortable. Not enough to ruin our plans or make us change our ways. Just enough to get by day to day without major crises or scandalous sins.

Yet we must consider the extravagant price Jesus paid to make God's grace available to us. He did not suffer unspeakable torments so that we could be comfortably selfish. He did not die a horrible death so that we could live a life wasted in petty pursuits. He did not vanquish the Devil in cosmic combat so that we could be free to do whatever we please.

No. Jesus, "the Pioneer of [our] salvation," suffered all this so He could bring us into the eternal glory of God the Father as true sons and daughters (Hebrews 2:10). The destiny He intends for us is nothing less than to "be like Him" when at last we "see Him as He is. And everyone who thus hopes in Him purifies Himself as He is pure" (1 John 3:2–3). Grace costs us everything, but in the end it makes us whole.

In this light, Maria's vision warns us against notions of cheap grace and calls us to embrace the Cross.

Many want to follow Christ, but only a few are prepared to imitate Him. No sooner do they feel the sufferings of the Cross than they throw it aside. In this way, many who are mortal, forgetting eternal truths, continually want to indulge the flesh and its pleasures. They fervently run after a great reputation and flee from insults; they wear themselves out for wealth and despise poverty; they pine for pleasure and fear discipline. All these are "enemies of the cross of Christ" (Philippians 3:18).

In addition, many who neither endure adversity nor exert themselves to be holy nevertheless imagine that they are following Christ their Master. They content themselves simply with avoiding the most brazen sins, and they consider themselves perfect if they attain a measure of prudence and an empty self-love. This attitude keeps them from denying themselves or from exercising any virtues that their flesh would find costly.

They would easily avoid such self-deceit if they would only keep in mind that Jesus was not only their Redeemer; He was their Teacher as well. He left to us in this world the riches of His redemption not only to save us from everlasting destruction in the next life, but also as a necessary remedy for the sickness of sin that afflicts human nature in this life.

No one was more capable than Our Lord of fulfilling His every desire if He had chosen to do so. Even so, though He could well have chosen to live a soft life, an easy life that made few demands of the flesh, He chose instead a life full of toils and pains. He considered that His instructions to us would be incomplete and insufficient to redeem us if He failed to teach us how to conquer the Devil, the flesh, and our own selfishness. He wanted to instill in us the truth that such a glorious triumph is gained by the Cross, by labors, by doing penance, by crucifying the flesh, and by accepting the scorn of men. All these are the signs and evidences of genuine love.

The Mystical City of God

*Lord, teach me to take up my cross daily
and follow You.*

40
To Live As Jesus Lived

He was despised and rejected by men; a man of sorrows, and acquainted with grief; and as one from whom men hide their faces He was despised, and we esteemed Him not. Surely He has borne our griefs and carried our sorrows; yet we esteemed Him stricken, smitten by God, and afflicted. But He was wounded for our transgressions, He was bruised for our iniquities; upon Him was the chastisement that made us whole, and with His stripes we are healed.

Isaiah 53:3–5

*B*oth Anne Catherine and Maria sharply condemned the wickedness of the historical figures who took part in the torture and murder of Jesus. But never in the visionaries' reports do we encounter self-righteous smugness. Instead, we hear the women's humble and repeated confessions, the bitter self-reproaches of two souls who were thoroughly convinced that they, too—though they lived many centuries after the fact—had a hand in Our Lord's execution.

The sacrifice of the Lamb of God, they knew, was a sacrifice for all time (Hebrews 9:26–28). His Blood, like His steadfast love and His faithfulness, extends to all generations, because all generations are in desperate need of its power (Psalm 100:5; Romans 5:18–19). The debt He paid was a debt that we all have incurred by our sins: "All we like sheep have gone astray ... and the Lord has laid on Him the iniquity of us all" (Isaiah 53:6). So each of us, by our wrongdoing, has played our own role in the passion story. Each one of us, at one time or another, has been a Judas, a Peter, a Caiaphas, a Herod, or a Pilate.

Were the visionaries simply indulging in the perverse pleasures of self-loathing? By no means! Both women recognized that "if we say we have no sin, we deceive ourselves, and the truth is not in us. If we confess our sins, He is faithful and just, and will forgive our sins and cleanse us from all unrighteousness" (1 John 1:8–9). Reflection on Our Lord's passion blossoms in contrite confession, which in turn bears fruit—not of self-hatred, but of divine pardon, and a renewed resolve to live as Jesus lived.

It is quite impossible to describe all that Christ, the Holy of Holies, suffered from these heartless beings; for the sight affected me so extremely that I became really ill, and I felt as if I could not survive it. My horror was as great as that of a murderer who is forced to place his hands upon the wounds he himself has inflicted on his victim.

Jesus endured everything without opening His mouth. And it was men, sinful men, who perpetrated all these outrages against the One who was at once their Brother, their Redeemer, and their God. I too am a great sinner, and my sins caused these sufferings.

At the Day of Judgment, when the most hidden things will be revealed, we will see the share we have had in the torments endured by the Son of God. We will see how far we have caused them by the sins we so frequently commit. Our sins are, in fact, a kind of consent we give to, and a participation in, the tortures that were inflicted on Jesus by His cruel enemies.

Alas! If we reflected seriously on all this, we would repeat with much greater fervor the words we find so often in prayer books: "Lord, grant that I may die, rather than ever willfully offend You again through sin."

The Dolorous Passion

Create in me a clean heart, O God, and renew a steadfast spirit within me.